THE
LEAN
TURNAROUND

**How Business Leaders Use
Lean Principles to Create Value
and Transform Their Company**

ART BYRNE

New York   Chicago   San Francisco   Lisbon   London
Madrid   Mexico City   Milan   New Delhi   San Juan
Seoul   Singapore   Sydney   Toronto

The **McGraw·Hill** Companies

9 10   QFR   21 20 19 18 17

ISBN   978-0-07-180067-9
MHID   0-07-180067-0

e-ISBN   978-0-07-180068-6
e-MHID   0-07-180068-9

Contents

Foreword

Art Byrne has learned more about creative change than any CEO I have encountered—many with big names—over the past 30 years. I know this because I have been following Art's work closely since we first met in the early 1990s when I decided to write about the Wiremold Company in Chapter 7 of *Lean Thinking*.

Art started his management career at General Electric more than 30 years ago, when it was widely perceived to be the best-managed large company in the world. As he recounts in Chapter 1, he soon learned the limits of what we now call modern management, the GE system of managing by results that has become a global norm.

Art then moved to Danaher, which with his help was to become the most consistently successful industrial company of the past 30 years. As group executive overseeing half of the Danaher portfolio of companies, Art played a critical role in making the company successful. He did this by learning from Toyota a new way to manage in which senior leaders took dramatic, direct action to transform core processes. This was codified in the Danaher Business System, which sustains an ever-growing company to this day.

Art then moved to Wiremold, where as CEO he learned how to rapidly transform every element of a large company, gaining knowledge as he went through a remarkable range of experiments conducted at his direction. He began by rethinking value from the standpoint of the customer and asking what leap in performance Wiremold needed in order first to survive (which was in doubt) and then to prosper. This went beyond the usual challenges of cost, quality, and delivery (all of which were successfully addressed) to asking anew about the problems that customers wanted Wiremold to solve.

One fact that became clear to Art almost immediately was that many customers did not want to buy isolated parts—the raceway and fittings needed for a building project. Instead, they wanted someone who could send a complete kit—with perfect quality at just the right time— containing all the parts needed to wire a scientific laboratory or a hospital or a factory. In addition, they wanted as much of the assembly of these parts as possible done at Wiremold before shipment so that whole wiring systems could be installed quickly, with minimum effort at the site. By rethinking value from the standpoint of the customer and creating new processes to provide this value, Wiremold was able to generate ever-growing sales at high margins in an otherwise stagnant industry.

Today, Art works in private equity, an activity that ought to be a major generator of wealth for society, but that often only shifts wealth from one group to another. Here he has learned how to transform a host of companies simultaneously, as the chair of their boards, in a way that creates more value for customers, stable jobs for employees, and new wealth for owners. In doing this, he has perfected a transformation model that can be followed by any CEO to redefine value and create growth even in depressed economies.

It is remarkable to find an individual who has transformed businesses at every level, from general manager of a business unit to group executive in a multibusiness company to CEO of a major manufacturing company to an operating partner in private equity overseeing a portfolio of companies as their nonexecutive chairman. But what really struck me as remarkable about Art from the day we first met 20 years ago was that he had the gift of making complicated things simple and engaging everyone in an organization in a crusade for dramatic transformation.

When I first entered Art's office at Wiremold in West Hartford, Connecticut, he immediately suggested that we take a walk together through Wiremold's value-creating processes to see a dramatic business turnaround in real time. As we walked, he described a remarkable vision of where he was taking the business by rethinking customer value and transforming the core value-creating processes, running across sales and customer support, product development, purchasing, and operations. I already understood most of what he was telling me from a technical standpoint. It was his ability to describe his turnaround methods in simple terms in the course of a short walk—and in a way that every member of the organization could understand—that I had never before experienced.

In this volume, Art describes in simple, clear language his learning journey to this new way of managing. Then—the truly important part—he tells CEO readers how they can achieve what he has achieved in any business if they are willing to roll up their sleeves, go to the *gemba* (the places where value is created), and learn from their own experiments.

This last part is hard for most modern managers because they have been taught that leaders can lead from the executive suite using business school theory plus PowerPoint, and that successful leaders never make mistakes. What Art teaches instead is that leaders must lead through hands-on experiments at the *gemba*, and that their mistakes—which are inevitable—will be accepted by their organization (including their board) if they are part of a rigorous transformation process for a clear purpose that permits everyone to learn.

As you read this book, you will hear Art's voice, with his distinctive way of making things clear and compelling. And you will hear a simple method for transformation of any organization in any industry. It is a method that is strikingly different from the counsel of today's typical business books, which are full of slogans and exhortations for heroic leadership, but which offer readers no useful guidance for navigating the interconnected world economy.

You will also hear a formula for making any society more competitive by starting at a molecular level in every organization, listening to customers, and creating the brilliant processes that must be the bedrock of great companies. This is also strikingly different from the financial engineering that has diverted managers in recent years and the government interventions that are often proposed in today's "competitiveness" debates. Instead, Art describes in simple, clear language his learning journey to a new way of managing that every reader with the courage to try experiments can follow.

James P. Womack

Founder and Senior Advisor at the Lean Enterprise Institute, Senior Lecturer in the Engineering Systems Division at MIT, and coauthor of *The Machine That Changed the World, Lean Thinking,* and *Lean Solutions*

Acknowledgments

This book, as you might expect, didn't just magically happen all by itself. In fact, it turned out to be a much bigger and longer project than I ever expected. Fortunately, I had a number of people who encouraged me and assisted me along the way, and I would like to acknowledge their contributions.

> *Mariko Byrne.* Mariko, my lovely wife and partner, provided the principal encouragement for me to even start this project. She stayed with it even when I got distracted and off track during the early going. She worked right along with me, typing all of my initial drafts (I can only type with one finger, so it is painfully slow) without complaining too much about my lousy handwriting.
>
> *Orry Fiume and Ed Miller.* Orry (vice president of finance) and Ed (vice president of marketing) are two of my former colleagues at Wiremold. They were our principal strategic thinkers, and I have always valued their opinions. Orry, in fact, had already written his own book, *Real Numbers*, with coauthor Jean Cunningham, and had a pretty good idea of what was involved in getting something on paper. As a result, I shared most of my early drafts with both of them and got a lot of very constructive feedback (both positive and negative). More important, like Mariko, they encouraged me to keep going.

Emily Adams. Once Orry figured out that I couldn't write very well, he introduced me to the editor of his book, Emily Adams. Emily was terrific to work with. She helped me to organize the flow and is a fantastic wordsmith. She could take my rambling explanations and quickly boil them down to the core essence of what needed to be said. She didn't like it when I called her the "word police," but she did a great job of getting me a manuscript that could be read by humans.

Jim Womack. I first met Jim almost 20 years ago when he was in the process of writing *Lean Thinking* with coauthor Dan Jones. We have stayed in touch ever since, and he is a sort of "intellectual godfather" of the Lean movement in the United States. Jim was a logical person to take my manuscript to. He gave me great encouragement and made a number of suggestions on how to make the book flow better. He also agreed to write the foreword and was a great help in the process of finding a publisher. He also introduced me to his longtime editor, Tom Ehrenfeld.

Tom Ehrenfeld. Tom has been instrumental in getting the book to its final state and in finding the right publisher. Not only has he had a lot of great insights and suggestions, but he has taken over the role of head cheerleader for this book. He has helped to keep me moving forward on this project and served as my main support structure in getting the project completed.

Mary Glenn. As the Associate Publisher for McGraw-Hill, Mary provided a lot of good advice and encouragement. More important, she led the way through the maze and coordinated all the right resources to get this book published.

INTRODUCTION

Any Business Can Be Turned Around

For most people, the idea of "turning around" a business conjures up certain types of activities: major head-count reductions, selling or closing the weakest parts of the company, selling off excess assets, reducing debt, increasing short-term earnings, and then selling the company. The idea of improving the way in which the company adds value in order to effect a turnaround never comes up. Why? I guess it is because most people associate the word *turnaround* with the type of financial engineering activities just mentioned. In addition, almost all companies, both good and bad, tend to take their value-adding activities for granted. The "this is the way we have always done it" mentality is alive and well in almost every company.

Yet if you step back and think about it, the way in which a company adds value is what distinguishes it from its competitors. It is, in fact, the most important and powerful way of succeeding in the long term. And so focusing on improving every value-added operation is where the true leverage lies. A real, sustainable turnaround for any company occurs only when it transforms each and every value-adding activity by removing the waste and letting value flow to the customer. In this way, any company, bad or good, in any industry, manufacturing or service, can be turned around—including yours.

Improving your operations (i.e., your value-adding activities) by relentlessly trying to find and eliminate the waste should be your primary, all-consuming strategic focus. Getting all of your people involved in this will not only greatly leverage your efforts, but eventually lead you to have a company culture of continuous improvement, or *kaizen*[1] (as Toyota would say). Once you get to that state, you will be very hard to beat.

There Is a Game Plan You Can Follow

I've learned that simply looking at how you create value in your company from a different point of view will open up possibilities that you would never imagine. And that's the point of this book: to show you how to create more with less. There is nothing hard here. All we need to do is change your focus to improving the value-adding parts of your business, and give you a few tools to help you see and remove the waste. I've gotten this done by using the Lean fundamentals first developed by Taiichi Ohno and his associates at Toyota.

I have been working on implementing Lean in various companies since the beginning of 1982. I have led or started Lean conversions in more than 30 different companies (or subsidiaries) spanning 14 different countries. My title has changed, but I have effectively led every transformation from the position of CEO. I wasn't the head of the *kaizen* office or a consultant or a continuous improvement (CI) specialist; I was a businessperson, just like you, trying to improve the results of the companies I was responsible for. I used a combination of Lean management along with some traditional management, and a lot of common sense.

The good news is that my approach has always produced exceptional results for all stakeholders. In 1987, George Koenigsaecker (who ran Jacobs Engine Brake as it's president) and I (in my role as group executive) introduced the Lean approach to the Danaher Corporation.

Since that time, Lean has played a huge role in the company's growth from $1 billion to $17 billion in size and in the way it is esteemed, being viewed as one of the most successful industrial companies in the United States. As CEO of the Wiremold Company from September 1991 until July of 2000, I was able to leverage the power of Lean to more than quadruple the company's size and increase its enterprise value by 2,476 percent.

I learned the Lean principles from four individuals at the Shingijutsu Company, men who had spent years working directly for Taiichi Ohno at Toyota. They taught me how they ran a *kaizen*, what forms and practices they used, and how to support Lean throughout the company. I believe that to be successful at transforming your company with a Lean strategy, you must adhere as closely as possible to this Toyota-developed approach. At the same time, I have developed my own method for managing the overall process. While my Toyota *sensei* taught me the Lean tools, learning how to combine all of them into an overall management approach was something that I had to learn through trial and error.

I remember early in our Lean journey at Danaher Corporation that George Koenigsaecker and I sat down with Yoshiki Iwata, the president of Shingijutsu, and asked a simple question: "How can Toyota allow other companies to learn about such a powerful strategic weapon as the Toyota Production System (TPS)?" (The term *Lean* hadn't been invented yet.) From the very beginning, George and I saw this as the biggest strategic advantage any company could have. Applied correctly, it had the potential to change everything—to make it so that no one could compete with you. Iwata's answer was very instructive. "I can teach you TPS," he said. "I can even show you TPS in action. But I bet you can't go home and do it." Over all these years, Iwata's simple insight has proved to be absolutely correct. Transforming your value-adding activities and your company's culture, and then leveraging these gains in the marketplace, is easy to explain but very hard to do. That's why you need a game plan that is simple, is repeatable, and works in any type of business.

And that's really what this book is about: leading the transformation of any company—manufacturing or service—by making better products with fewer resources, and saving jobs by finding the true value of an enterprise, reliably and repeatedly, through Lean thinking. Then, leveraging those gains in the marketplace to create wealth and better personal outcomes for all your stakeholders.

Make a 180-Degree Turnaround

While Lean strategy is based on the simple notion that you will never be successful if you continue to ignore your value-adding activities or take them for granted, this idea is almost the exact opposite of what most of us have been taught about modern management. As a sign of how backward our current set of assumptions is, most of us spend a lot of time trying to get our customers to conform to the way we do things instead of trying to configure ourselves to be responsive to the customer.

In fact, the modern management approach tends to focus on everything *but* the value-adding activities when looking to improve the company's results. Service companies, for example, will usually install a new computer system (at great expense) rather than actually fixing the way in which the work itself gets done—which results in nothing more than automating the waste that exists, not removing it. For manufacturing companies, the focus tends to be on developing new products, investing in capital-intensive automation, or, more recently, outsourcing the actual value-adding work to some low-cost supplier in China.

The entire modern management philosophy is strongly reflected in the forecasts that I see in the private-equity business as we look at new companies to buy. In most cases, you will see projections that show a flat to gradual rise in margins over time, and also in key balance sheet metrics like inventory turns. Big increases are sparked only by management's assumptions about a new product or new market that will change the company's mix. Rarely do you see any forecast that contemplates gains (either in margins or in market share) from fundamental changes in the way in which value is created. As a result, while traditional companies can grow and pass on wealth, they are not very good at creating wealth by becoming productive in everything they do.

A good example here is a service company that takes 20 to 30 days to respond to an application for one of its products with a quote. The competition responds in 18 to 20 days. This company knows that it is on the high side, but all the people in the management chain have bought into all the excuses as to why it can't reduce the time. Their response is to introduce either new products whose features will overcome the company's slow response time or an expensive new computer program (with no guarantee of success) to bring the time down. The company sells through a network of agents and brokers, each of whom typically carries four or five competitive products. So, the opportunity is very clear. If the company could utilize the Lean tools and improve its value-adding to the point where its turnaround time was only 10 days, it would be able to dominate its market. New products would just be a bonus. The problem, of course, is that most companies just can't see the strategic advantages of improving the value-adding activities.

Change Your Vision

In order to help you turn your company around, I have to be able to get you to see things differently. You have to develop "Lean eyes" so that you can see the waste that is clogging up your value-adding activities. If, for example, I walked around your factory or office with you, I would see opportunities everywhere that you can't see. Don't worry; you won't be able to change your vision overnight, but if you follow the approach I have laid out, you will get there fairly quickly.

If you are a manufacturing company, the biggest obstacle to letting value flow is long setup times. Therefore, one of the first goals in a Lean transformation is to cut your setup times and keep reducing them to the point where they are all in single digits (under 10 minutes). Fortunately, this is pretty easy to do, and it is not capital-intensive. The biggest

Table I.I   Some *Kaizen* Results: Setup Times
Reduction During a One-Week *Kaizen* event

Equipment Type	Setup Time (minutes)		% Reduction
	Before	After	
Rolling mill	720	34	95%
150 ton press	90	5	94%
P.M. punch press	52	5	90%
Hole cut on mill 1228	64	5	92%
2½˝ extruder	180	19	89%
Injection molder	120	15	88%
Average Setup Reduction = 91%			

hurdle you will face is the resistance from your middle management, engineers, and setup men. They will have a long list of reasons why nothing can be done to cut your two- or three-hour setup times. To help you overcome these objections, I have provided the chart in Table I.1, showing the setup time reductions we achieved at Wiremold on a range of different types of equipment over the course of one week each. The average reduction is 91 percent. Oh, and by the way, this was just the start. For example, the injection-molding machines eventually got down to setups that were between one and two minutes.

When you have low setup times, everything changes. You can actually connect the customer directly to the production cell and its value-adding employees. This new link increases the employees' sense of purpose, boosting their understanding of what the company has to do to satisfy its customers. This also reduces costs, improves quality, dramatically shortens lead times, and greatly improves customer service. This, in turn, will allow you to gain market share and grow faster than the industry average.

But don't think that this applies only to manufacturing! Similar opportunities exist everywhere. Consider service companies. Here the waste in value-adding activities is often hidden by the organizational structure that has been put in place and grown over the years. Each fiefdom has some form of specialty function that only it can perform (that is, according to the people involved). Let's say we are dealing with a loan application at a bank. The application has to go through six different departments, located on six different floors of the bank, in order to finally get approved or rejected. The applications move from one floor to the next a couple of times a day. If one lands on someone's desk and that person is in a meeting all afternoon, it waits until tomorrow. Or if it lands on the desk of someone who has taken a couple of vacation days on Thursday and Friday, then it will sit until Monday. Adding up all the possible delays, it may take three to four weeks on average to process the applications.

But what if we thought about value-adding differently? We know that the mail, with all the loan applications in it, is delivered daily at 10 a.m. and 2 p.m. What if we got one person from each of the specialty fiefdoms (departments) and sat them around a big table? We would then dump the mailbag next to the first person, and the people could just pass the applications around the table until they were done. The process would now take closer to three minutes than three weeks. And if the volume of applications rose, we could add another table or two, or work on how to make the first table flow faster (i.e., increase productivity).

Either way, switching to focusing on improving the value-adding activities in response to the demands of the customer will have a dramatic impact on the value that you can return to the customer—not to mention what it does to your costs, the amount of space you need, and your quality. Just think of the competitive advantages that being able to turn around a loan application in two days will give you relative to the three or four weeks that it takes all your competitors. It could make a great ad for local TV, for starters. You would be swamped with business.

The key, of course, is to get you to understand the advantages of flow rather than batch[2] for your value-adding activities—not just to increase your output, but above all to give you the tools that will allow you to "see" the opportunities yourself and a method for how to exploit them. This book will take you through that process step by step.

These are only two examples, but switching to a Lean strategy can help any business. For example, many hospitals in the United States are making great strides in implementing Lean; Virginia Mason Medical Center in Seattle, Washington, and Thedacare in Appleton, Wisconsin, are two of the leaders. But the principles can be applied to help any business. Including yours.

Create More with Less

How powerful a financial tool is Lean? Let me illustrate with some results that I have witnessed, and that are pretty standard for what you should expect.

Every year I take about 20 managers from our portfolio companies to Japan for a week to tour factories—including Toyota—that are well advanced on their Lean journey. The purpose of this trip is to let them see firsthand "how high is up." Most of the individuals have had quite a bit of Lean experience in their own companies, but until they see for themselves what is possible, they have no sense of how far they have to go. Several years ago on this trip, we had just finished a tour of a first-tier Toyota supplier. In the Q&A session with about eight of the supplier's managers, we learned that it had only two days of total inventory (raw, work-in-process [WIP], and finished goods). When I stood up to thank them with my closing comments, I mentioned that the four companies represented in our group had between 70 and 80 days of inventory each. Once this was translated, it set off a lot of chattering and looks of disbelief among our hosts. They couldn't believe that anyone could possibly have that much inventory. On our side, of course, as I pushed everyone to improve his inventory turns, it was very helpful to take them where they could see what two days of inventory looked like compared to what they had at home. It was pretty hard for them to continue to argue that they couldn't get inventory much lower.

So what should you expect from using Lean management and strategy to turn your company around? My experience, and that of many others, would suggest that for manufacturing companies, you could achieve, at the least, the following results:

- Lead times cut from weeks to days.
- Inventory turns doubled in two years and quadrupled in four.
- Annual productivity gains of 15 to 20 percent.
- A 50 percent reduction in defects per year.
- A 50 percent reduction in floor space in two years.
- A 4 to 8 percent improvement in gross margins.
- Working capital as a percentage of sales cut in half.
- Increased growth by taking market share.
- The creation of a team culture in which every person can learn and create personal wealth.

These are certainly not the end points of what you should expect, but they are pretty typical of what other companies that have implemented Lean in a serious way have achieved. In other words, at a minimum, you should plan to achieve these targets. How high is up for your company is up to you. As a hint, you can do much better than these guidelines. (Look at the Wiremold results in Chapter 1 for more details.)

If you are a service company, perhaps some examples from another service company would be more instructive to you in getting an idea of what type of results are possible with Lean. In this case, I have used CHG Healthcare Services, one of our J. W. Childs Associates, L.P., portfolio companies. CHG is the largest privately held healthcare staffing company in the United States. It is the leader in physician staffing (locum tenentes) and a leading provider of travel nurse and allied health staffing. Like all J. W. Childs portfolio companies, it has been using Lean principles to improve its value-adding activities and thus grow its enterprise value. From 2006 to 2011, revenues and EBITDA (earnings before interest, taxes, depreciation, and amortization) have grown at a compound annual rate of 6 percent and 14 percent, respectively, despite a severe recession in its market in 2009 and 2010. Lean has played a key role in this by:

- Reducing the time required to respond to a physician inquiry from 25 hours to 26 minutes, which greatly expanded its base of physicians.
- Cutting accounts receivable days' outstanding by 10 days, freeing up $16 million in cash.
- Running *kaizen* events that eliminated 24 steps in a key customer process, cut the time to fill physician openings by 22 percent, and produced estimated annual new revenue of $2.5 million per year.
- Helping a client reduce physician credentialing time from 84 days to 42 days—a 50 percent improvement.
- Reducing the amount of time from getting an assignment to presenting a credentialed candidate by 84 percent.
- Reducing net debt outstanding by 38 percent in 12 months.

The point is that employing a Lean strategy can transform any company and produce great financial results.

How You Can Start Your Lean Transformation

Getting from here to there is a challenge. Few companies and their leaders see the full potential of Lean to transform their business. Most people see Lean as some "manufacturing thing," and so they simply make it one element (usually a minor one) of their overall strategy. Lean gets delegated to operations and gets an increasingly narrow focus on cost or inventory reduction. This greatly reduces its effectiveness. It also helps explain why only about 5 to 7 percent of the companies that attempt to implement Lean do so successfully. They are doomed before they even start because they see it as only operational and not strategic.

I know that you will face many challenges, including a great deal of resistance. So I hope that this book will provide you with the courage to get started. I know that the conversion to a Lean strategy can't be managed in the traditional way. It can't just be delegated down. The CEO must lead it in a hands-on, out-front, in-the-*gemba*[3] (workplace) way. If the CEO won't change his ways and become totally engaged (become the company's Lean zealot), then there is little, if any, chance of turning any company around using the Lean principles. The focus has to be on creating value, not on cutting costs.

What I hope to do with this book is share what I have learned with you so that you can lead your own Lean conversion. Yes, you will have to learn a few key Lean tools, and you will have to participate in many *kaizen* projects. But the more important part of this book is about getting you to think totally differently about your value-adding activities— essentially, about the way you work. And in order to help you change the way you and your colleagues work, I hope to help you understand the resistance you will face, and help you to overcome it so that you can lead (not manage, but lead) your team to success.

So let me start by sharing how I learned about Lean, and then I'll lay out a simple method for you to put it to work.

My Lean Journey

I started out just like you: a traditional management guy. My first exposure to Lean at GE was very small and narrow, but the strategic implications were huge. I wanted to do more, but I needed to learn more first, and at Danaher, I was fortunate to be able to work with the experts from Shingijutsu, who helped me understand how to start kaizen. I learned this approach in depth by forcing myself to be on lots of kaizen teams. I was the group executive, and I could have avoided this by delegating the kaizen work to someone else. That would have been a colossal mistake—and one that I hope you don't make. As a result, by the time I got to Wiremold and J. W. Childs, I knew not only what to do but how to go about it, how to lead it, and what the strategic implications were for big gains in value creation—that is, enterprise value.

Make the Month Meets Lean at General Electric

When I joined General Electric in early 1980, it was known as one of the best companies in the world, and it was the recognized leader in strategic planning. Even so, it was hiring people with strategic planning backgrounds to bring new perspectives and enhance its internal approach. I was hired as a strategic planner in the Lighting Business Group. Three days after I got there, my boss was put on a special assignment, and I became the de facto head of planning for the group.

At the time, GE was a very traditional manufacturer. Its management approach was top-down, manage the numbers, aided by a strong central financial group. We pretty much had a single measurement focus on earnings: make the month or die. Jack Welch had become CEO not long after I arrived, and he added a lot of energy, along with being a great leader and a strategic thinker. The company was full of bright, aggressive individuals, an environment that challenged you to learn things quickly.

Even so, despite all the positive management approaches, I found an equal number of practices to be wasteful. For example, the capital appropriation process was big and bureaucratic. It even had a full-time staff at the corporate level to review the big projects. This meant that getting something approved took three to six months, even though few changes to the original request were ever made. In addition, our focus on detailed reviews of the numbers each month meant that management spent 8 to 10 days each month reviewing (or preparing to review) what had happened last month. More important, the balance sheet was taken totally for granted. However, since I had a traditional batch background, I didn't really have a basis on which to question this until I was introduced to Lean.

At the beginning of 1982, I got my first general manager's job at GE as head of the High Intensity and Quartz Lamp Department. My operations manager, John Moffa, had just returned from a trip to Japan to study just-in-time manufacturing. The trip was sponsored by corporate manufacturing, and John had to give a report in six months about something he had implemented as a result of the visit. Jim Grimes, who was head of operations for one of the Lighting Business Group's component manufacturing departments and a big supplier to my business, was also on the trip. As a result, John and Jim decided to set up a simple *kanban*[1] delivery system between two of our plants that were about 45 minutes apart. The product focus was the expensive quartz arc tubes that we used to make our high-pressure sodium lamps. John and Jim bought a van that delivered to my factory every day. Each order was based on the quantity and type of tubes we had used the day before. We used a simple visual system, *kanban* cards, to indicate what was needed. Each box of arc tubes had a *kanban* card. As a box of tubes was used, the attached *kanban* card, equal to one box of tubes, was collected and given to the van driver to indicate what was needed the next day.

At the time, I hadn't had much exposure to Lean. I was a traditional management guy, but this approach made sense. So I said go ahead, as did my counterpart, Gary Carlson, who ran the supply business that made my arc tubes. Gary and I outlined this idea to the other general managers of the Lighting Business Group during a staff meeting. They laughed. They said that all that would happen was that I would end up transferring my inventory back to Gary, and the overall impact on the group would be negligible. We couldn't argue with them because we had no real Lean experience. But we didn't like being laughed at, so we just went ahead and made it work.

Quartz tubes are costly little parts. Within about three months, my inventory of those parts dropped from 40 days to 3 days and stayed there. Customer service improved too, because while we did not have many tubes, we always had or could quickly get the right ones. Six months later, Gary Carlson asked me to visit his plant where the quartz arc tubes were made. He said it was important, so I drove out there. He greeted me warmly and took me to a large empty room in his factory. "What's this?" I asked. "This?" Gary said. "It is not just an empty room. It used to be full of quartz tubes that we made for your business. We no longer keep any inventory. We make them each day based on the *kanban* cards that you send each morning."

Not only had my inventory dropped by 93 percent, but Gary had eliminated his inventory completely. Then we took a walk around and compared notes. Both factories were cleaner and much neater; there was more space. It was easier to find the right arc tube. With fewer tubes available, people became more careful with them, and breakage went down, as did defects. Productivity improved, lead time improved, and customer service improved. Workers on the shop floor told me that they were happier—they were proud of their work area. All we had set out to do was create a simple pull system using *kanban* cards, but the side benefits were so good that I was hooked.

The more Lean work I did, the more apparent it became to me that simple changes in the way in which value was added could create big results. The year 1982 was a recession year in the United States, and my sales dropped about 20 percent. There was no way I could make my budget. Even so, the reduction in inventory was so great that I was able to deliver better cash flow than the year before despite the drop in sales. The problem was that in a "make the month or die" world, no one cared. Somehow that didn't seem right to me.

GE at that time represented a "best-in-class" example of the modern management approach. Lean was 180 degrees different in terms of where you focused your energy, but it was fundamentally simpler and better. In my future roles, I made sure that I did not take the wasteful aspects of the GE approach with me. My exposure to Lean had really opened my eyes. GE, by the way, eventually added some balance sheet aspects to its incentive system. It also adopted Six Sigma (an unfortunate diversion, in my opinion), and several years ago, it got more serious about Lean. What I don't know is whether "make the month" is still at the core of its culture.

I wouldn't trade my experience at GE for anything. Through this work, I learned how simple changes to the way value is added provide multiple ways to improve financial results. I saw the ways in which dramatic amounts of inventory can come out of the value stream, and I learned that the steps you take to reduce inventory are the things that will improve your earnings and your market share. And I learned how focusing on improving your processes will give you better future results than wasting time reviewing last month's results. I was able to build on these lessons in the next stop in my Lean journey.

Learning *Kaizen* by Doing *Kaizen* at Danaher

I joined the Danaher Corporation as a group executive (one of two) at the end of 1985. I was responsible for 8 of the then 13 Danaher companies, and my counterpart, John Cosentino, was responsible for the other 5 (although we split the $1 billion in sales about 50–50). Our office was in one of my subsidiary companies, Jacobs Engine Brake (Jake Brake), in Bloomfield, Connecticut. Our total staff was one assistant, whom we shared.

I had appointed George Koenigsaecker as president of Jake Brake not long after I arrived. George K. (as we always called him) was the only other person at Danaher with any prior Lean exposure at that time. He took over a business that was a mess—a business that we both wanted to use Lean to turn around. (By the way, the term *Lean* hadn't been invented yet; we called it just-in-time or the Toyota Production System.)

The Jake Brake plant was a heavy machining operation making engine brakes for heavy-duty diesel trucks. The floors were covered with oil, and the factory was dirty everywhere. The workforce was represented by the UAW. We made good progress, and pretty soon we had our first cell, the CAT cell (it made engine brakes for Caterpillar's class 8 diesel engines). In the process of forming this cell, we moved a lot of equipment into a U-shaped configuration so that the product could flow from machine to machine without delay. George K. and his team cleaned and painted everything as they went (the walls, the ceiling, the floors, and the machines). We even put some potted plants and new lighting in the cell to really make it look different. It looked great, and it was clearly the right idea. The problem was that it didn't work very well. In fact, there were days when it didn't work at all. In the previous batch operation, the machines had never really been maintained (fix it when it breaks was the idea), and they often went out of tolerance as well. This gave us a lot of trouble, but we were convinced that this was the right approach, and we never even thought of going back to the old ways. George K. and his team just dug in to fix the problems.

Several months after the CAT cell was up and running (well, sort of running), George K. noticed a seminar that was going to be held in Hartford, Connecticut, run by Masaaki Imai, the author of the book *Kaizen*. George K. signed us up, and I attended the seminar with several of his key people. I could stay for only the first two days, but by that time it was clear that the consultants that Imai was using to teach the seminar, the Shingijutsu Company from Gifu, Japan, were the real deal. All of them had worked directly for Taiichi Ohno, the father of the Toyota Production System. George K. pursued this aggressively. He took them to dinner and then to the plant at about midnight. They almost caused a riot.

I was able to meet with them one afternoon later in the week when they visited the plant again. When we asked them what they thought, they just said, "50 percent"—meaning a 50 percent reduction in everything: people, space, defects, lead time, inventory, and so on. They later told us that they had said 50 percent because they didn't think we would want to hear the real number.

We were hooked, but it took a lot of pushing by George K. to finally get them to agree to come help us. They started with Jake Brake's sister company, Jacobs Chuck (also one of my companies), and Jake Brake at the same time. We were their first U.S. clients.

Our new guides introduced us to the Toyota approach to running a one-week *kaizen*, including all the paperwork. We ran multiple teams every time they came and spent the periods in between their visits trying to do the follow-up work necessary to maintain the gains. George K. and I participated in many full-week *kaizen* teams. Shingijutsu's approach was that you could learn only by doing, and this was correct. (This will be true for you as well, as we'll discuss later.) We didn't just visit the teams during the week; we worked with them full time. It was the only way to learn how to use the *kaizen* tools to solve problems.

We had problems similar to those I mentioned for the CAT cell almost every time we set up a new cell. I don't want to give you the impression that this was easy. But George K. and I were convinced that the *kaizen* approach to changing how we added value in the company (from batch to flow) was the correct way to go, so we stuck with it. And Jake Brake enjoyed tremendous success. We freed up more than half the floor space, cut lead times from more than a month to days, improved quality, reduced inventory by about 70 percent, and enjoyed productivity gains of just under 30 percent (in terms of engine brakes per man-hour) per year for about seven years in a row.

Of course, one of the side effects of a rapid drop in inventory is that you lose the overhead absorption benefits that you get when you build or maintain inventory levels. This happened at Jake Brake, and you should expect it, too. The better we got at adding value, the worse our P&L looked in the short term. Eventually this resulted in a "special emergency" visit of the Rales brothers (the owners of Danaher) to see what was going on. George K. and I decided that bringing them straight up to the conference room to discuss the numbers would be a big loser for us. Instead, we felt that we should first take them out on the shop floor and show them the changes we had been making. George K. even went a bit further and had the shop floor tour conducted by the UAW workforce, who could tell them with a lot of pride what had happened in their work area. Well, this was brilliant. The tour lasted about three hours (George K.'s team had accomplished a lot by then), and when we got back to the conference room, there was no financial review. To their credit, all the Rales brothers said was, "Wow, how fast can you do this in the rest of the Danaher companies?"

This was great (we were still employed!), but when we asked the Shingijutsu consultants to expand into the 11 other Danaher businesses, they refused. They said Brake and Chuck were still so bad that they wanted to get them in better shape before they would help us elsewhere. Our solution was to create the presidents' *kaizen*. First, we took all 13 presidents and their vice presidents of operations to Japan for one week to tour factories and see the Toyota Production System at work in other companies. Next, Cosentino and I essentially ordered the presidents and their VPs of operations to participate in a three-day *kaizen* (we couldn't coordinate their schedules well enough to do a five-day *kaizen*) in one of Cosentino's plants every six weeks. By then, George K., a few of his people, Dennis Claramount, president of Jacobs Chuck, a couple of his people, and I had been on enough *kaizen* teams with Shingijutsu to be able to act as the consultants for these presidents' *kaizens*.

During the very first presidents' *kaizen*, we killed a $750,000 capital appropriation request for a new paint line that was in the final stages of approval. Another team was able to go from 14 people to 3 people and get the same or slightly better output. These events were fun, and we got a lot done. We would be moving sizable pieces of equipment by early afternoon of the first day. Not only did we achieve great financial results from these *kaizen* projects, but we started to build a great camaraderie among the presidents. This led to a *kaizen* culture in Danaher despite the fact that no 2 of the 13 companies were in the same business. We believed that if we couldn't get the presidents to buy in and push *kaizen* in their own companies, then we wouldn't get too far with it in Danaher. This was true then, and it will be true for you as well, by the way. We forced our presidents to do *kaizen*. You are going to have to force yourself.

The more *kaizen* I did myself, the more I understood the financial leverage that could come from changing the way we added value on the shop floor. This was very clear to me early on. George K., John Cosentino, and the Rales brothers also understood the strategic leverage here very quickly. Surprisingly, though, most people didn't make the connection easily. It was far more common for people to look at anything that happened on the shop floor as just some "manufacturing thing." As a result, I found that my role as group executive changed dramatically the more *kaizen* we did. I went from the more traditional role of managing the numbers every month to spending most of my time leading the way forward.

My visits to my various operations always started with a walk on the shop floor to see what progress had been made since my last trip. I organized and led a lot of *kaizen* projects just to make sure people got it. I left a lot of homework to be done before my next visit (mostly physical changes in the way value was added or reductions in setup times or freeing up space and lowering inventory). I also set a lot of stretch goals to make sure we were moving forward.

This change in my management approach wasn't something that I spent a lot of time thinking about. It sort of happened naturally the more I learned about *kaizen* and how to change the way value was added in order to remove the waste. I'm sure this will happen to you as well. At the same time, I can guarantee you that this approach is a lot more rewarding, both personally and financially.

Leading a Complete Lean Transformation at Wiremold

Founded by D. Hayes Murphy in Milwaukee, Wisconsin, in 1900, Wiremold moved to West Hartford, Connecticut, in 1929, into a brick factory tucked up in a modest neighborhood. D. Hayes Murphy was the son of an Irish immigrant who had arrived in the United States in 1859 with one dollar in his pocket, having lost $99 playing cards on the boat on the way over. The elder Mr. Murphy, Daniel E. Murphy, became a successful insurance agent and tried to get D. Hayes interested in that business, without much success. D. Hayes was more interested in making something tangible, so in 1900, with his father's backing, he bought a small firm that manufactured electrogalvanized metal conduit.

While he was building the company, D. Hayes had three daughters and two sons, and he treated his company as a true family business. He expected a good day's work for a good day's pay, but he was willing to share success with all employees. He established a profit-sharing program in 1916 that designated 15 percent of pretax profit to be shared with all employees. Murphy's two sons, John and Bob, kept that profit-sharing program in place when they took over from their father—John as CEO and Bob as president. By the time I arrived, profit sharing had become embedded in everyone's idea of Wiremold. The company was unionized, but profit sharing was kept out of the union contract.

As John and Bob reached retirement age, they passed on the CEO job and active management of the company to their chief financial officer, Warren Packard. Warren epitomized the smart, honest approach that had been established by the Murphy family. By 1991, Packard was ready to retire.

During Packard's tenure, the company experimented with Lean's precursor, just-in-time production, with fairly disastrous results. The idea behind just-in-time, the managers were told, was to consider the inventory as water in a pond, and to lower the level throughout the company in order to expose and then fix the "rocks." Eventually, as the rocks were fixed, batch processing and huge inventories would simply disappear. That was the theory. The problem was that there was no reliable, consistent method for fixing those rocks. Inventory fell too low to keep customers supplied with products in a timely fashion, problems in the manufacturing process were not getting fixed, everyone was stressed, and orders were not being filled. Just-in-time—*that Japanese approach*—developed a terrible reputation. Wiremold fled back into batch production, relying on even larger batches and more inventory to fill customer orders.

On the plus side, the family atmosphere created by the Murphys meant that people liked working at Wiremold and truly cared about the company. My new staff was a group of very bright, dedicated managers, so I did not have to come in and clean house. I knew from my prior experience at Danaher that the best ideas for improving a process always come from the people who are actually doing the work, so I was blessed from the start with a group of good people.

The trick, of course, was getting them to look at things differently. Most people do not like change very much, and many are afraid of it. For Wiremold to be successful, everything had to change. When I got there, the company had no growth, and earnings had declined by more than 80 percent over the past two years.

As the only person at Wiremold with experience in the principles and methods of the Toyota Production System, I knew that I would also have to be head salesperson for the new approach. I would have to lead by example, out on the shop floor—the *gemba*. (For some reason that I cannot fathom, many executives still seem to believe that value is created in their executive suites; they spend all their time there, and then wonder why they are disconnected from their companies, or surprised at quarterly results.)

To help with this, I created a Lean manufacturing methods manual and trained the first 150 people. I picked the first *kaizen* events, assembled the first teams, and led them on the shop floor. I set the targets for each *kaizen*. I worked on embedding in Wiremold's workforce three simple ideas that would be fundamental to our adoption of Lean:

- Productivity equals wealth.
- Focus on process, not results.
- Teamwork across the entire company.

Working with the staff, I reorganized the company into value streams and picked the value-stream leaders. Each value-stream leader had full responsibility for a product family (i.e., a value stream) and was given all the equipment necessary to make the products in that family, from raw material to finished goods. Functional departments were dissolved. If a value-stream team leader needed steel rolled and plastics molded to finish his product, he was given rolling mills, injection-molding machines, and the people necessary to operate them. We did not buy new machines, but reassigned the ones we had. Team leaders were judged by process driver measurements (such as inventory turns, quality, productivity, and on-time delivery) that were part of our strategy. I also introduced outside consultants to help run *kaizen* projects, create one-piece flow, and train our people in aspects of the Toyota Production System. The consultants did no formal classroom training. Instead, they taught everyone how to "see" the waste in any process and how to remove it during *kaizen* weeks.

Changing a factory from batch processing to flow is a tremendous undertaking. Most likely, every process will need to be redesigned and re-laid out—most of the time more than once. This means moving a lot of shop floor equipment. At Wiremold, we had punch presses, rolling mills, plastic extruders, plastic injection-molding machines, and several major painting systems. Once we started the Lean conversion, we were moving equipment across floors and between buildings on an almost-daily basis. At the same time, we were making small alterations to many machines and tools to facilitate quick changeovers. For example, we had 1,600 punch press dies, and each one had to be altered to a common shut height.

This explosion of activity was quite a shock for our people. So were the expectations. When we did our first rolling mill setup reduction *kaizen*, for instance, everyone on the team thought I was out of my mind when I said that we were going to reduce the 14-hour rolling mill setup time to less than 10 minutes. We had to do a number of *kaizen* events and alterations to this mill, but several months later, when the setup was down to 6 minutes, I no longer seemed crazy, and I had a new crop of energized believers. And that is a critical key for any leader: use stretch goals and improvement teams to sell Lean to your people. Think strategically about who needs convincing and when, and put that person on a high-impact team.

When it came time to pick the team for one of our first *kaizen* projects, for instance, I asked Orest J. Fiume, the chief financial officer, to join the setup reduction team for a punch press. Orry was not just a great CFO, he was a very bright guy who saw everything in a common-sense way. He had the respect of other members of the senior team, and I needed him as a Lean believer. He did not go gently onto that team, however. Orry was busy; Orry said he knew nothing about machine setups. Eventually, he acquiesced. In the course of one week, Orry's team cut the punch press machine setup from 90 minutes to 5. Ever the finance person, Orry kept track of how much we spent doing this. It was about $100. This was his aha moment. From then on, he became a true believer and a tremendous help in getting others on board with a Lean approach. Eventually, he would take Lean principles into finance and revolutionize management accounting. Retired from Wiremold now, Orry is the coauthor of a very popular book on Lean accounting, *Real Numbers*, and spends his time running seminars and doing lectures on Lean and Lean accounting throughout the world.

As we got better at *kaizen* projects and swept up more of the money that was lying around the factory floors in the form of excess inventory, we also paid closer attention to what our customers wanted. Our service levels improved. We developed new products and acquired a number of our smaller competitors. Profit-sharing levels increased for the workforce, and employee performance improved every year. *Kaizen* became the way we did business at Wiremold, and how we thought about problem solving.

Every part of the company, from sales to human resources to manufacturing and finance, was involved and part of the new *kaizen* culture.

We closed the books at the end of the month like everyone else, but we did not use the numbers to manage the business. Results were something that had already happened; it was too late to do anything about those numbers. Instead, we focused on creating better processes in order to improve our future results. My staff and I performed a weekly (eventually biweekly) review of value-stream team leaders to see how the process drivers (such as customer service, quality, productivity, inventory turns, and visual controls) were measuring up, and how *hoshin* team leaders were doing on new product development or other strategic initiatives.

Once we had a Lean culture at Wiremold, it turned out to be relatively easy to convert the companies that we purchased to our Lean strategy of continuous improvement. Wiremold employees had become true believers in Lean. And once you have that kind of momentum, your people become the true drivers of the improvement culture.

During the 1990s, while everyone else seemed to be rushing at investment bubbles and exploding high-tech stocks, this is what we did at Wiremold:

- Lead time dropped from 4 to 6 weeks to 1 to 2 days.
- Productivity improved by 162 percent.
- Gross profit improved from 38 percent to 51 percent.
- Machine changeovers went from 3 per week to 20 to 30 per day.
- Inventory turns improved from 3 times to 18 times.
- Customer service improved from 50 percent to 98 percent.
- Sales grew from $100 million to $400 million.
- Earnings before interest, taxes, depreciation, and amortization (EBITDA) margin improved from 6.2 percent to 20.8 percent.
- Working capital/sales fell from 21.8 percent to 6.7 percent.
- Operating income improved by 13.4 times.
- Enterprise value increased by 2,467 percent (from $30 million to $770 million).

For a serious Lean conversion led by dedicated people, these are typical results. I experienced similar gains in the eight companies I was responsible for at Danaher, all of which underwent Lean conversions.

Any Company Can Be Converted to Lean

I retired from Wiremold in July of 2002. But I flunked retirement and joined J. W. Childs Associates L.P. as an operating partner shortly afterward. J. W. Childs is a middle-market private-equity firm based in Boston, and I joined as part of Fund III, which is $1.9 billion in size. The founder, John Childs, started the firm with the concept of having full-time operating partners in order to make sure that we could grow and improve the companies that we invested in. This is quite different from most private-equity firms, which mostly employ pure finance types. The approach certainly proved its value during the 2008–2010 recession.

John Childs himself is one of those rare individuals who was able to grasp the strategic implications of Lean right off the bat. Not only could he understand the gains from changing the way in which value is added, but he could extrapolate that into the kind of gains this would mean for our portfolio companies, and consequently for our investors. As a result, we have been implementing Lean in all of our portfolio companies, with great success. John has been a great leader in this through a combination of pushing all the CEOs forward and also through his hands-on Lean activities. He has come with me on the annual one-week visit to Japanese factories, and he spends about two to three full weeks per year on *kaizen* teams in our various factories.

At J. W. Childs, I have mostly implemented Lean from the position of chairman of some of our portfolio companies. Most of these companies come into the portfolio with an existing CEO who has no Lean experience. Sometimes we can get a CEO to buy in and lead the conversion to Lean, but other times we can't. With the four companies I have been chairman of, I have had to replace two of the CEOs to get a better push on Lean, and I have recently gone through a transition with a third in which the longtime CEO retired and we made sure that his replacement came with strong Lean credentials. We know the value that Lean can bring for our investors, so we can't afford to wait too long to get traction on the Lean conversion.

At J. W. Childs I function a little like I did as a group executive at Danaher Corporation. We use outside consulting help to bring the Lean knowledge to our companies. In addition, I set the agenda and goals as well as the measurement process for my companies. I also develop the bonus targets and the weighting of the elements that make up the bonus. I lead by example by running a lot of *kaizen* projects on the shop floor. Getting each management team aligned behind Lean as its strategy is the primary focus. Once this occurs, we can make rapid gains in all the key financial areas, especially in enterprise value.

For our overall portfolio, we have gotten significant Lean gains in many nonmanufacturing companies as well as in those that manufacture. For example:

A leading sales and marketing company:

- $8 million in savings and efficiency gains

A major anesthesiology provider:

- Accounts receivable (A/R) days outstanding: down 31 percent
- A/R processing errors: down 50 percent
- A/R productivity gains: up 30 percent

A specialty retailer saved $563,000 by:

- Improving picking by 40 percent
- Cutting incoming product inspection time by 33 percent
- Processing customer returns 50 percent faster

A major healthcare staffing company:

- Cut A/R days by 10, freeing up $16 million in cash

A mattress retailer:

- Cut time to open a new store by 9 days
- Reduced merchandise returns by 43 percent
- Cut time from site tour to real estate approval by 20 days
- Cut inventory by $2.8 million
- Reduced delivery costs by $550,000

A beverage manufacturer:

- Consolidated from three buildings to one building, saving $5.2 million
- Developed a Lean to Green Program that:
  - Lowered energy consumption by 18 percent
  - Reduced water usage by 25 percent
  - Cut calories by 30 percent, saving $8 million

A private-label razor manufacturer:

- Had a six-point increase in EBITDA margins
- Tripled inventory turns
- Sold for 3.5 times the investment

A couple of the companies where I am chairman are also showing strong gains. In one, we sold a major division three years after we bought the company. This allowed us to return 1.1 times their money to all investors and pay down all the debt. We were left with a $1 billion company with only $15 million EBITDA in 2005. Since then, we have doubled down on our Lean efforts and freed up more than $100 million in cash, and we now have a $1 billion company earning $90 million in EBITDA. In another company, which is still very much in the early stages of Lean, we have increased EBITDA margins by 4 basis points, improved inventory turns from 9 to 20 times, increased working capital turns from 6 to 108 times, and cut setup times by more than 40 percent. With continued progress on Lean, I expect at least a 3 times return from this company.

My experience in private equity has confirmed my belief that you can improve the value of any company and make a lot of money by using Lean management and Lean strategy. It's taught me that if the CEO doesn't buy into Lean, you need to act quickly to replace him to avoid suboptimizing your investment return. And it has taught me that a strong push from the company's owners and its board goes a long way toward ensuring success. My Lean journey has taught me these lessons, and more.

In the rest of this book, I would like to teach you the steps to take and the mindset you'll need in order to be successful as well.

Don't Just Do Lean; Be Lean

Using Lean to turn your company around has a very simple focus. You want to improve all your processes so that you vastly improve the way value is added in your company. Doing so will increase both your market share and your enterprise value. This can occur only if you understand that Lean has to be your strategy— the foundational core of everything you do—if you are to be successful. Lean is not a "manufacturing thing." Lean is a strategic approach that covers everything you do. And so you can't delegate the change or try to manage it. You have to lead it in a visible, hands-on way. Most important, you have to understand that the main thing you are trying to transform is your people. They are the only asset you have that appreciates in value. All the best ideas to improve will come from the people who are doing the work, not from you. Always treat them with respect.

In order for your Lean turnaround to be successful, you will have to understand and commit to three management principles that will serve as the foundation on which your transformation will be built:

- Lean is the strategy.
- Lead from the top.
- Transform the people.

In my 30 years of transforming companies using Lean thinking, the most common reason that I see companies fail is a lack of one or more of these principles. They all need to be in place for you to be successful.

Lean Is the Strategy

Prior to the 1970s oil crisis, very few people in the world knew what Toyota was up to. The fact that it emerged stronger than ever while many of its competitors were quite battered made people take notice. People went to Japan to find out how Toyota had done this. What came back was that Toyota was doing something called "just-in-time." In the West, this was interpreted as an inventory reduction program. As a result, it became known as the "just-in-time inventory" program. Nobody really believed that inventory could be taken out of the whole value stream, and so "just-in-time" came to mean "just-in-time inventory; go beat the heck out of your suppliers." The Big Three auto companies had lots of power over their suppliers, and they became pretty expert at this tactic—to their own eventual detriment.

Then James P. Womack and Daniel T. Jones published *Lean Thinking* in 1996 and helped us to see the whole value chain. They showed how waste clogs the system, and how continuous improvement was needed to link all parts of the chain to customer demand. The authors explained their findings in plain English, but once again, we did not hear. We somehow managed to ignore the whole system aspect of Lean thinking and started calling it "Lean manufacturing" instead. This tragic reduction in scope allowed business leaders to dismiss Lean as a "manufacturing thing." As a result, manufacturing companies believed that Lean could be delegated down, and nonmanufacturing companies believed that Lean didn't apply to them at all. Even today, the uninformed perceive Lean as a bunch of tools that can be used selectively. In most companies, Lean may be an element of the larger strategy, but it is most likely to be relegated to the plant. As a result, one company after another has tried Lean and has failed.

The truth is, Lean is the most strategic thing you can do to transform your company. Perhaps a simple example will help. Let's assume that Company A and Company B are competitors. They buy the same equipment from the same vendors and use it to compete against each other. The only difference is that Company A takes one hour to change over its machines, whereas Company B (without big capital spending) has figured out how to do it in one minute. If the two companies can each afford to dedicate only one hour a day to setup, then which will have the lower costs and which will have the better customer service? Company B, of course, on both counts, but the real question is, is this strategic, or is it just some "manufacturing thing"? How can Company B build on this advantage? If the industry lead time is six weeks, but Company B can use its rapid setups to offer a two-day lead time, it will certainly gain market share. And how will Company A then respond? Most likely it will either build more inventory (worsening its cost disadvantage) or cut prices, which will further erode profits. Company B, however, can use its greater speed and responsiveness to continue to gain market share without cutting the price. Does it sound more strategic now? All we did was cut setup time—something that most people see as a "manufacturing thing"—and we realized a huge strategic advantage (i.e., lower costs and better customer service). And that's just one crucial way to illustrate that improving the way value is added in your company is the most strategic thing you can do. It is the enabler for any other strategic moves you may want to make.

I realize that this is a hard concept for most people to grasp. Throughout your career, strategy has meant big-picture ideas or dramatic moves to gain advantage in the marketplace. No one ever thinks of improving value-added as part of strategy. But using Lean to improve all your processes (for example, to achieve lower costs, better quality, shorter lead times, and better customer service, plus freeing up lots of space and cash to reinvest for future growth) will profoundly boost your ability to execute on what you now consider to be "strategic" initiatives. And you will create a wealth of new strategic options (such as offering a two-day lead time while the rest of your competitors are still at six weeks) that you would not have even seen as possible before changing your value-adding approach.

For those who came up in a make-the-month world, as I did at General Electric, the idea of focusing on process instead of results may be hard to swallow. Everyone wants to improve his company's results. I have found, however, that the best way to reliably improve your results is to fix your processes. Spending a lot of time analyzing what happened last month—as happens in a traditional company—is a waste. Last month already happened. You can't do anything about it now. Companies that focus on the past usually try to offset bad results from operations with some wizardry in accounting (think Enron, Health South, or WorldCom), but they are rarely successful for long.

What you can affect is the present and the future, and improving your processes now means that you will have better results next month, and the month after that. Better results come from delivering better value to customers. This is the essence of what any company's strategy should be: delivering value to customers. People get confused here and talk about strategies such as "enhancing shareholder value." This is looking at strategy backwards. Shareholder value will increase only if the company can deliver superior value to customers on a consistent basis over a long period of time. So, shareholder value is a result, not a strategy.

Switching to a Lean strategy, by the way, doesn't mean that you have to give up doing all the things you have historically thought of as strategy. You can still try to develop new products, enter new markets, and improve your quality and your customers' experience. The difference is that switching to Lean will allow you to execute these actions much faster and more economically. You will be able to do things that your competitors can't do. You will have the strategic advantage.

Think of Lean as a time-based growth strategy. The steps you take to improve your value-adding processes will automatically reduce the amount of time it takes you to do everything. Companies that compete on speed will naturally gain market share against slower competitors.

More important, history has proved that people will pay for speed. Think of FedEx taking business away from the U.S. Postal Service. The post office still charges less than a dollar to reliably deliver a letter anywhere in the country, as long as you do not mind waiting. FedEx collects an enormous price differential (more than 2,000 percent) based on the promise of getting it there fast.

Never lose sight of your main objective in making the Lean transformation: delivering value to the customer. Do not begin a Lean transformation in order to cut costs or reduce inventory or achieve some other internal goal (which, unfortunately, is the most common approach). Lean cannot be just one of 10 elements of your strategy. It must be the foundational core of everything you are trying to do; that is how it becomes your culture.

Don't just do Lean; be Lean.

Lead from the Top

Conceptually, shifting from a traditional to a Lean strategy is simple and straightforward. The problem is that it is very hard to do. The reasons are twofold. First, shifting your existing structure (your physical layout and all your systems) into a Lean configuration where you can see and eliminate all the waste will take a very big multiyear effort. And second, you will face resistance (very strong resistance) from your people at pretty much every level. Therefore, implementing a Lean turnaround cannot be delegated down in the organization. Without your strong leadership pushing everyone forward to improve all your processes in order to reach your financial goals, not much will happen. Even if you make some gains, the overwhelming tendency is to go right back to the old way. I have never seen this not happen. It can be overcome only by a strongly determined leader with a clear set of goals (vision) who is actively driving the change.

Part of leading the change is leading by example. You can't send out a memo or give a few brief speeches and think that things will change.

All organizations are used to "flavor of the month" improvement ideas and are expert at quietly waiting each one out until it goes away. Switching to Lean is a major physical and cultural undertaking. It will take years before you can even start to think you will be successful. As a result, you have to lead by example so that your people know that you are serious and committed. You also have to be the one that keeps the whole change effort on track when things start to drift back to the old ways.

In smaller, privately owned companies, for example, the CEO should be on the floor actively participating in *kaizen* events on a regular basis. Six or eight one-week events per year would be a good target. The same holds true for small to midsize public companies. This can be harder to do as the size of the company goes up—say, for businesses with more than $2 billion in annual sales—but the CEO should still participate in *kaizen* events at least once a quarter at the most critical facilities. Also, think about appearing at *kaizen* wrap sessions via video-conferencing. Being a Lean leader means getting involved in details that may have been overlooked before, like how the company produces value. Knowing the details intimately will enable the CEO to set key goals with authority, and to encourage staff members to stretch toward goals that are more difficult. To do this, you must understand what is possible, and for this, there is no substitute for being on *kaizen* teams. The more Lean expertise you gain, the easier it will be for people to follow your lead. You do not need to start out a Lean expert, but you must commit to becoming one.

My Japanese teachers had a wonderful expression for this. "Byrne-san," they told me, "if you don't try something, no knowledge will visit you." This was part of the learn-by-doing philosophy that is so critical to becoming a Lean leader. The typical CEO is going to say, "Gee, I'm the CEO. Why do I have to become a Lean expert? I can hire someone or use a consultant for that." This is clinging to their traditional management approach where this is the way things are done: give orders, hire the expertise you need, and stay out of the nitty-gritty.

Unfortunately, as with everything else in Lean, the approach to leadership is 180 degrees different from the traditional way. For example, to remove the waste from all your processes and improve the way your company adds value, you first have to be able to see and understand just how much waste exists. If it takes three weeks to process a mortgage application that could be done in less than two hours, wouldn't you want to know that? Similarly, if a job that now takes 10 people could be done with 3 (without any capital spending), aren't you interested in that?

This is what being on a lot of *kaizen* teams and learning the lean tools will teach you. If, for example, you are on four teams, and each time you achieve a 60 percent drop in defects, a 50 percent productivity gain, a 50 percent reduction in floor space, an 85 percent reduction in lead time, and, if you are a manufacturing company, a 75 percent reduction in inventory, what is your reaction? Don't you think you would be starting to gain some insight into the waste that exists in your company? Wouldn't you also be starting to understand how easy it is to remove the waste by improving the way you add value? Well, this is what I am talking about, and it's why you need to commit to becoming a Lean expert. The more you know, the more waste (i.e., opportunity) you can see. In addition, the more you know, the easier it will be for you to break down the barriers to change and improvement that currently exist in your organization. Most important, the more you know about your value-adding activities (i.e., how bad they are), the more willing you will be to set the type of stretch targets that are necessary if you are to be the leader in your industry. One thing is certain: if you don't have a goal of being number one, you never will be.

And make no mistake: Lean will change the leader. As we got more advanced in Lean work at Danaher and Wiremold, my approach to my job changed significantly. I became more of a coach and a leader, and less of a manager. My focus shifted completely to where we were going and how we could get there, rather than where we had been. I spent all my time encouraging and pushing people to achieve things they might not have thought were possible. There was no better feeling than seeing a team exceed a target that at first seemed impossible.

In essence, I changed from spending a lot of time reviewing last month's results to focusing on all the processes in each of my various businesses. Yes, I looked at the numbers each month, but I didn't conduct any formal reviews of them. If a couple of managers' costs were out of line, I would talk to them and get them back in line. Most of my time, however, was spent trying to make sure that we were making steady progress toward achieving all of the stretch goals aimed at process improvement. I spent a lot of my time on the shop floor looking for what had changed and reviewing the visual control charts at each cell. When I visited one of my companies (I had eight at Danaher, between eight and twelve at any given time at Wiremold, and up to four or five at a time at J. W. Childs), I started on the shop floor so that I could see what progress had been made since my last visit.

My discussions with managers and employees at all levels were focused on our value-adding activities. Why couldn't we go faster? Why weren't the visual controls up-to-date? Why hadn't setup times come down more? I spent a lot of time saying "no good" when I saw things on the shop floor that could be improved. I always left a lot of homework to be done before my next visit, and of course all the targets were stretch in nature. My main concern was making sure that everyone on the team was on board and driving for the same goals.

If you are going to lead, it is imperative that you know that people are following. You could string me along for a little while, but because changes to the value-adding activities tend to be physical in nature, this wouldn't last long. I would be able to see the lack of progress on my next visit. You either got on board or went away.

This approach, by the way, didn't mean that I was some kind of ruthless dictator. In fact, the opposite is more accurate. I was seen as part of the team, but with the role of coach. Everyone felt free to approach me with any questions or concerns without fear of recrimination. I encouraged this openness, and our associates really took advantage of it. They asked a lot of good questions and made a lot of good suggestions that I always tried to follow up on. At the same time, they always understood that I was pushing them to get better. They were okay with that. It was just part of the deal. They knew that when I stopped for half an hour to observe some operation, I was looking at the work (the sequence and the way we had it organized), not the worker, and I was thinking of ways to make it better. I always tried to explain to them what I thought was wrong and why we should make it better.

Watching how the workforce responded to changes in the way work was done was always rewarding. People who were very vocal about not wanting to change at first, saying, "This Lean stuff is stupid," would, three or four weeks later, be your best advocates for doing even more. Similarly, teams that took setup times from 90 minutes to 5 minutes or from 180 minutes to 1 minute were more than just a little proud of what they had done. The fact is that being a hands-on leader is much more rewarding than being a traditional manager. Making the Lean turnaround will force you in this direction, so go with it. You will be glad that you did.

Transform the People

As CEO of your company, you have many assets at your disposal. Only one of those assets, however, has the ability to appreciate over time: people. In a truly continuous improvement environment, the best ideas will always come from the people who do the work. In fact, the traditional structural hierarchy pyramid that puts the CEO at the top should be inverted, placing the frontline, value-adding people at the top and the CEO at the bottom. If you are not contributing to helping the value-adding people do their jobs in an easier and better way, then you are just waste. Unfortunately, the traditional command-and-control management approach does not recognize this, with the result that a company's most important decisions are usually made far from where the value is being added. This tends to create a check-your-brains-at-the-door atmosphere that vastly underutilizes people.

I don't think any company sets out to take any less than full advantage of its human resources. Unfortunately, the traditional management approach has a very strong tendency to inadvertently do exactly that. The extreme focus on "make the month" doesn't leave a lot of room for suggestions coming from the employees. Even when they do make suggestions, they are often ignored, or the response is so delayed that they get the message and stop offering advice. But if you can accept the idea that people are your most important resource, then this doesn't make much sense. You will have a much stronger and better company if you are fully utilizing the brains of your entire workforce. If, for example, you have 1,000 employees, wouldn't you be better off getting ideas from all 1,000 rather than just relying on the top 30 to 50 people in the company all the time?

In a Lean transformation, this tendency to underutilize your people is reversed. This is true because the only thing you can really transform is the people. Sure, you can move equipment around, close facilities, cut setup times, and reorganize your office layout, but transforming the way your people think and act is the real key to success. It is just human nature for people to become set in their ways when it comes to work or how they solve problems. First-line supervisors are so pressed to make their numbers that they don't have time to listen to employee suggestions.

With Lean, however, you want to get all the suggestions you can from your value-adding employees, and you want to implement them as soon as possible. The *kaizen* approach of a dedicated team working on a problem for a whole week gives everyone a voice. Ideas for improvement are implemented on the spot. The change for your value-adding employees is immediate and dramatic. All of a sudden there is an organized company approach, with dedicated resources and the strong backing of the CEO, to try to make their job better. After all the waste is removed, the job will be safer, easier, and take less time. All of this translates into more output with less effort on the employees' part, and they get it right away. At Wiremold, we reduced many setup times from two to three hours to one to two minutes. Our setup men contributed most of the breakthrough ideas, and we made sure those ideas were implemented. Everyone gained, and everyone was happy.

A great illustration of this occurred a few years into our Lean journey at Wiremold. We had been asked to give a presentation on Lean to a major AME (Association of Manufacturing Engineers) conference. We chose a setup reduction where we had gone from 320 minutes down to 1 minute. Because most of the best ideas had come from the two setup men, we decided to have them make the presentation. They were very nervous about this, but we helped them prepare and had them focus on the major changes ("I used to have to crawl under the machine, and now I don't") that were made. At the end, they showed a one-minute video of the changeover. The first comment from the professional engineers and managers in the audience was, "Gee, Carlos, you looked like you were going pretty fast in that video." Now, we had not rehearsed this at all, but Carlos didn't miss a beat. He looked at the guy with a quizzical look on his face and said, "Yeah, but only for a minute." It was perfect.

The Lean focus on removing waste creates a learning environment for everyone. It leads to great teamwork, which in turn creates a great work atmosphere. The focus on being responsive to customer needs naturally builds a customer-centric organization where everyone is participating. People like coming to work every day in this type of environment. They are constantly learning new ways to improve your value-adding activities. In essence, the Lean organization understands the value of its people and treats them with great respect.

Now while *kaizen* will be your major tool in transforming your people, there are a lot of other simple things that you as CEO can do simultaneously that will help your turnaround. At Wiremold, I began my tenure with a promise that nobody would be laid off as a result of Lean improvement work. When I said this, it seemed that there was a collective gasp from management and union representatives alike. *The CEO was offering a job guarantee without extracting some other concessions from the union in return?* I explained that this promise had nothing to do with contract negotiations. I was making the promise because it was the right thing to do, and everyone needed to know that his job was safe as he helped us improve productivity. Union environments, by the way, are no more difficult than nonunion environments when it comes to implementing Lean. Just treat everyone the same way you would like to be treated and you will be fine.

I also made sure that all my communications to all associates were clear and simple. I got rid of the practice of management wearing ties (cuts off circulation to the brain) to try to build the "we are all in this together" teamwork that we needed. I also made sure that I was honest in response to employees' questions, even when I knew that they wouldn't like the answer. At the same time, I always tried to explain *why* we were doing something so that everyone understood the rationale.

To try to get everyone on the same page, I asked Judy Seyler, vice president of human resources, to create a more user-friendly code of conduct: a few simple ideas that would fit on a single page and tell everyone who we wanted to be. Her team came up with this:

> **Wiremold Code of Conduct**
>
> Respect others
> Tell the truth
> Be fair
> Try new ideas
> Ask why
> Keep your promises
> Do your share

This was posted on the walls in every facility, laminated on wallet cards, and handed out to everyone. We talked about the code of conduct at quarterly employee profit-sharing meetings, and we emphasized our commonality. This is a critical piece of the Lean people work, I believe, because for all of us to be moving in the same direction, each of us needs to know what is expected. Besides the standard admonitions seen in most codes, ours also promoted a Lean, team-based culture. By "keep your promises," we were talking about doing *kaizen* follow-up work on time. By "do your share," we meant that implementing Lean requires teamwork and nobody should be allowed to fall behind. By "ask why," we were saying that we expect everyone to challenge the common wisdom so that we can move past the current state and improve.

We also were able to reduce the number of job classifications that we had from about 50 to 5. This was necessary to create the type of flexible workforce we needed in order to implement Lean and improve the value-adding work. If you can go from ten people to three to do the same job, the three have to be multiskilled. To be honest, this took us some time to implement, but it added to our sense of teamwork and gave us a chance to give our employees a lot of new skills. We made sure that no one was hurt financially as we consolidated the job classes.

A company in which people are truly respected gives everyone the opportunity to grow as the company grows, and to share in the wealth that is being created. The 401(k) plan was the biggest single shareholder when we sold Wiremold, and therefore the employees got the biggest share of the wealth that was created. For everyone, the objective is to make Lean and continuous improvement the core culture of your company. When Lean is your culture and every associate is part of the team that creates and delivers value to your customers, you will be very tough to beat.

Lean Principles to Guide Your Transformation

In order to lead a Lean transformation, you need to learn and implement four fundamental principals: work to takt time, create one-piece flow, establish standard work, and connect your customer to your shop floor through a pull system. These Lean fundamentals are straightforward. However, they have little chance of taking root in your company without your insistence and total commitment. Making it happen is up to you.

So how do you get started? At this point, I would expect that you might be asking yourself a couple of questions, namely:

- How do you expect me to lead a Lean revolution in my company if I don't know much about Lean myself?
- How much knowledge will I need before I can use Lean to transform my company?

These are the right questions. Leading a Lean transformation is hard work, and needs your leadership if it is to succeed. But don't worry. You don't have to do anything heroic to lead a Lean transformation. I led many while I was in the process of learning Lean, and you can do so too. In fact, I hope to make it easier for you by pointing out the critical things you need to know so that you won't waste a lot of time.

The Lean fundamentals that we discuss in this chapter are the basic things you need to know. They will do two things for you. First, they will allow you to see the waste that exists in your company in a way that you can't do now. This is important because if you can't see the waste, how will you convince the rest of your team that it's there? More important, they will serve as your guiding principles throughout your transformation. It is critical that you learn and internalize these Lean fundamentals.

Lean Principles

For Taiichi Ohno, the Toyota executive who drove the creation of the Toyota Production System, Lean had two foundational principles: continuous improvement and respect for people. Continuous improvement means a lot more than looking for ways to improve. Ohno said that improvement should actually become the focus of the organization, and that improvement over the long term should always trump short-term considerations. Companies that truly respect people, he said, listened to their employees' ideas for improvement and implemented them.

In *Lean Thinking*, Womack and Jones defined Lean principles as having five parts: identify value, map the value stream, create flow, establish pull, and seek perfection. This was the unceasing circle of improvement work that every company should engage in, they said, beginning with identifying the real value that is being offered to customers and then removing all waste that stands between that value and the customer.

Womack and Jones also popularized the term *Lean* to describe Toyota's system of continuous improvement. This was an important step, as it helped people realize that this approach could be applied to any type of company (which would not be the case if you called it just-in-time or the Toyota Production System [TPS], both of which had manufacturing connotations). All companies should be striving to deliver value immediately in response to their customers' demands without wasting any resources (make what is needed, when it is needed, and in just the amount needed).

In fact, the more waste you remove, the faster you will be able to respond to your customers.

From these broad concepts and my experience, I have distilled what I consider to be Lean fundamentals. In essence, what we are trying to do is remove the waste so that we can get to a state of continuous improvement. There are all kinds of Lean "tools" that have been developed to make this happen. They sound a little like alphabet soup sometimes: SMED, 5WHY, 5S, 3P, poka-yoke, KPO, and so on. While all of these can help you, there are four Lean fundamentals that will serve as the foundation for your Lean transformation. These are the most important things for you to learn. If you master these four fundamentals and relentlessly drive them into your company, you will be able to turn your company around successfully. They are:

Lean Fundamentals

- Work to *takt* time
- One-piece flow
- Standard work
- Connect the customer to the work by using a pull system

Takt Time

Takt time represents the rate of customer demand and therefore the desired rate of production. The term *takt* is a German musical term meaning "beat" or "measure." Lean practitioners invoke the metronome when talking about *takt*, to illustrate a steady pace, and it is one of the most important elements of Lean. *Takt* keeps everyone's attention focused where it needs to be—on the customer.

You can't start an improvement activity without first knowing what the *takt* time is. You need to go only as fast as the customer demand. Anything faster would be waste. When I ask the question, "What is the *takt* time?" at the beginning of a *kaizen*, what I am really asking people to determine is what we are really trying to do. At what rate do we have to produce in order to meet customer demand?

This is a concept that applies to every business. When I led a Lean turnaround at Saint Francis Hospital, the first *kaizen* we ran was in the cathology lab. When I asked what the *takt* time was, the staff members of course just looked at me like I was from Mars. Once they understood, however, it was the key to ending all their overtime and staffing problems and freeing up about $500,000 per year in extra revenue for the hospital. It allowed them to see where the real waste was and to organize a flow and a form of pull system to get patients in and out of the labs faster, with less waiting and downtime.

Takt time also applies, say, to order entry. Almost all businesses have some form of order entry, but if you went in and asked the people doing it what the *takt* time was, they would have no idea what you were talking about. If you asked them to calculate the rate at which they have to enter orders, they would say that you can't do that. Their rationale would be that some orders have only three lines and others have three hundred, so the time required to enter each is highly variable. But if you understood what the average order size was and how many orders per day there were, then you could calculate the *takt* time. When you apply that to what they are actually doing, the overstaffing would shock you.

As an equation, *takt* time is:

$$\text{Time available/daily customer demand} = takt \text{ time}$$

So, for example if we have 450 minutes of working time in a day—typical for a one-shift, 40-hours-per-week operation—and customers are ordering 450 units per day, *takt* time is one unit per minute. At this relatively slow rate, most producers will have a lot of flexibility in selecting equipment for production. For instance, a few inexpensive benchtop machines or several simple machines linked together might work better than those high-volume monuments. One operator may be able to complete the operation, moving between machines. This simple setup should be easier to change over. The important idea is to let *takt* time (i.e., the rate of customer demand) guide every aspect of production.

Of course, customer demand will fluctuate because of seasonal demand patterns or growth in market share. Let's say demand rises to 900 units per day. *Takt* time is now 30 seconds instead of 60, and you may need to either add a second operator to your low-cost line or create another identical production cell. The investment matches customer demand in this case, instead of trying to force customer demand (through sales, rebates, and the like) to meet your excess capacity.

Connecting your production rate to your customer through *takt* time is critical, but to complete the picture, you also need to know the cycle time—the rate at which products are produced. What you are trying to do is to get the cycle time to match the *takt* time. When you have done this, you will be responding to customer demand in the way that has the least waste. Making the comparison between *takt* time and cycle time is also the approach that will allow you to start to be able to see and understand the waste that exists in your business.

Let's say that there are seven steps in the process for making Product A, and there are seven operators working on Product A. The operators are in seven different functional departments across the factory, but they are dedicated to making Product A. We can go from one operation to the next, timing how long each step takes, and then comparing total cycle time to *takt*. This might look like Figure 3.1.

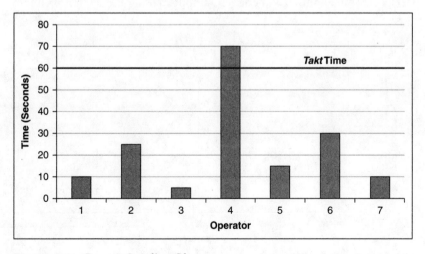

Figure 3.1   Percent Loading Chart

Comparing cycle time to *takt* time tells us that this operation cannot meet customer demand, because production can move only as fast as its slowest step. One operator, Operator 4, will have to work overtime, at added cost, or the plant will need to carry excess inventory to avoid customer service issues. The chart also tells us that the other six operators are underutilized when compared with the *takt* time.

Adding up the cycle times of all the operators gives us a total cycle time of 165 seconds to make Product A, compared to a *takt* time of 60 seconds. For efficiency, each operator's cycle time should equal the *takt* time. So, divide the cycle time by the *takt* time to see that 2.75 operators are needed to have the cycle time equal to the *takt* time (165 seconds ÷ 60 seconds = 2.75 operators). Assuming that you have pulled each of the seven processes out of its functional area and colocated the work in a single cell, you now have the flexibility to adjust the operators' work content to have them meet the *takt* time. Operator 1 can be given enough work to bring him to a 60-second cycle time, as can Operator 2. Operator 3 can do the remaining work and still have 15 seconds to spare (see Figure 3.2). This is a 61 percent productivity gain. All you did was compare the cycle time to the rate of customer demand (*takt* time), and you were able to "see" something that had been hidden from you before. There is nothing quite like *takt* time in a traditional manufacturing or service company environment, so without making the switch to Lean,

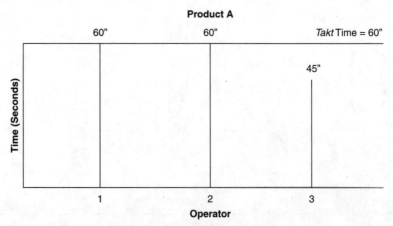

Figure 3.2   Reconfigured Percent Loading Chart

you would have never gotten this productivity gain. But, even that is not the true benefit.

Keep in mind that this Lean conversion is strategic. You want to compete on operational excellence and time. The true strategic insight from this exercise is the fact that touch-time labor to complete Product A is 165 seconds, yet the current process has a six-week lead time. Comparing *takt* time to cycle time allows you to see strategic opportunities that you couldn't see before. Now you know that you can offer a one-day lead time and use that advantage to capture market share. Every time a competitor stumbles, you can offer shorter lead times and pick up the business at full-book price.

Customer demand, in the form of *takt* time, should be prominently displayed at every product cell, along with information on how the cell is performing relative to *takt* time. Display this large enough so that a quick walk around the factory or office will tell you instantly whether you are meeting your customers' needs. In this way, you can connect the customer directly to the shop floor. You want to get to the point where every cell meets *takt* time every day. Then you know that you are meeting 100 percent of customer demand every day.

In summary, the concept of *takt* time is a powerful strategic weapon. It allows you to see the waste and the strategic opportunities. It also provides the basis on which you can now think about connecting your customer directly to the work cell, thus eliminating the need to carry big inventories (just-in-case).

One-Piece Flow

The 61 percent productivity improvement that we discovered in the previous example can be achieved only by rearranging the steps in the process from functional departments to one-piece flow (see Figure 3.3). In one-piece flow, the operations are placed in sequence right next to one another, and every piece of work in process (WIP) moves smoothly from one step to the next until it is completed. Think of a mortgage application being handed from one specialist to the next until it is either approved or

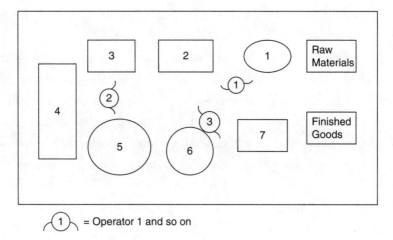

 = Operator 1 and so on

Figure 3.3 One-Piece-Flow Cell for Product A

rejected. Each application will take only minutes to process, as opposed to the current system, where it takes three to four weeks because it needs to travel between different functions on different floors.

Not only does one-piece flow reduce throughput time, but it is also the key to big gains in quality and productivity. Once the new cell with three operators (rather than the previous seven) is established, we can observe the entire process visually. We can see whether one operator is working at a different rate from the others. We can also see bottlenecks in the process or places where the operators are having trouble or moving in awkward ways. Solving these problems should allow us to go from three operators to two. We want to focus the operators on doing only value-added work at the *takt* time. We don't want them doing material handling or running off to look for tools or parts. Everything should be at their fingertips. We can use a material handler (which we call a water spider) to supply parts in small quantities to this cell and probably to several other cells as well, as shown in Figure 3.4. This will further enhance our productivity and quality.

Once a product or product family is in a one-piece-flow cell, it is much easier to determine its cost, at least down to the contribution margin level. You know the material content, the labor, the floor space, and the disposables used in production. More important, you can see

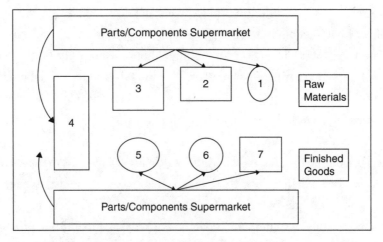

Figure 3.4 Parts and Raw Material Flow for One-Piece-Flow Cell

when you are having problems in a cell (it will shut down completely) and begin to implement fixes long before your accounting system would ever indicate that you had a problem. Your planning systems are also greatly simplified. In the old traditional layout, you had to figure out how to move parts and pieces between seven functional departments that were spread out all over the building, and coordinate them in such a way that four to six weeks later, you made a blue one or a red one. Now you can just say, "Make me a blue one," or, "Make me a red one," and you can have it in a few minutes.

When it comes to quality, the move to one-piece flow usually means at least a 10 times improvement—at no cost. There is a simple explanation for this. When things are made in a batch (i.e., when they travel from department to department or office to office) over the course of four to six weeks, defects are often not seen until final assembly. But when did the defect occur? What department, what shift, what machine, or what individual is responsible? Or maybe it's a material problem. But, you buy from three different vendors, and it is impossible to tell their materials apart. Of course, adding four to six weeks of time between the event and its discovery doesn't make the job any easier.

Once this operation is moved into a one-piece-flow cell, however, all these issues go away. First of all, there are only seven steps in the process, so we will find the problem very quickly. In addition, we now know what machines were used, who the operator was, and whose material it was. This gives us a high likelihood of not only finding the problem, but creating a permanent solution. Oh, and as a side benefit, we will have to throw out only a few defective products or parts, whereas we would be looking at scrapping four to six weeks of parts with the traditional approach.

For your people, the switch from functional departments to one-piece flow is quite a change. The good news is that once they adjust, they generally like the one-piece-flow approach better. Before, they may have worked on only one component part and never seen the finished product at all. Now they are part of a small team that makes the complete product, from raw material to a packaged finished product, and they take great pride in that. More important, once a one-piece-flow cell is established, it gives you a place to which you can directly connect the customer demand (something that is impossible to do with a functional layout). This means that your operators can not only take pride in making the complete product, but also be proud that they are meeting the customer demand.

Standard Work

Standard work refers to the standard way in which any value-adding job (the work) needs to be done. Everyone who is doing this job needs to do it in the exact same way (i.e., the standard work). The standard work encompasses the work, the work sequence (Step 1, Step 2, and so on), the tools needed, the equipment needed, the materials, and the amount of time it should take. Standard work certainly needs to be in place for every value-added job, but it can also be used in other areas as well. What should be the standard work for a sales call, for example?

Establishing standard work is extremely important for your Lean transformation. It is the basis for all improvement. If I don't have a standard way of doing a job (one that is adhered to), how will I know whether I have improved or not? Also, if I don't do the job the same way every time, how can I get consistent quality or productivity? More important, without standard work, how can I be assured of keeping up with customer demand without having to carry a lot of inventory?

Standard work can be established step by step as you do *kaizen* on various value-adding activities. When you set up a new one-piece-flow cell, for example, you have to establish standard work for every operator in the cell, and also for the water spider that supplies the cell. This should be written down and posted at every workstation so that every person knows the job, the work sequence, and the time for each task. Use pictures or illustrations if you can to make it as clear as possible. If you are doing a setup reduction, you need to establish standard work for that as well. If the standard work is done correctly and posted at every station, this should allow you to train a new employee (or someone who is just filling in for the day) very quickly. This will give you a lot of staffing flexibility as your volume moves up and down throughout the year. Once standard work is established, the important part is to make sure that everyone follows it.

For most companies making the Lean transition, getting people to follow the standard work is the hard part. The reason is that their prior way of working was so different. If you observed five people doing the same job in a traditional environment, I can almost guarantee you that no two of them would be doing it the same way. In fact, even the same person may do the job in a slightly different way each time. This is because the focus in this environment is usually just on the end result, not on how you did it. "We need to make 1,000 pieces today." As long as we got 1,000, everyone is happy. Not only the workers but line management as well sees this as okay.

As a result, getting people to follow standard work will be one of your biggest challenges. It is probably the hardest part of making the Lean transformation. It can be achieved only if the CEO insists on it and follows up religiously. You can help yourself out here by making sure that every *kaizen* team has on it an operator and a supervisor from the area that the *kaizen* is focusing on. This will allow them to understand the standard work that was created and spread the word to the rest of their team.

Connect the Customer to the Work—Pull System

The final Lean fundamental links back to *takt* time in its focus on the customer. Simply put, a *pull* system is one in which customer demand is what sparks the activity that makes the product to satisfy the customer's desires. In a push system, you make a thing based on a forecast and push it out to the market, hoping that a customer will buy it. This system disconnects the factory, which produces only to a forecast, from the customer. A good pull system allows the customer to tell us what to make and when, thus guaranteeing the sale.

The basic pull concept is very simple: when you sell one, make one. If you don't sell one, don't make one. It begins with the customer and then backs up through production, where the user goes to get—or pull—parts from supplier operations in just the amount needed, only when needed. This continues all the way back to raw material suppliers so that every segment of the business, from grower or miner to consumer, is tied together like links of a chain.

The principles are simple, but I have to warn you that implementation is hard. Even Toyota struggled with this in the early years. Only after establishing one-piece flow and standard work—and after the whole operation is working to *takt* time—can most companies initiate a true pull system. Oddly enough, most companies that try to implement Lean do it in exactly the opposite way. They start with a pull system and mostly skip the rest. They still batch everything, and they still have loads of inventory. But now they have *kanban* cards on all their excess WIP and think they are Lean. I have seen this many times.

Still, a pull system is a fundamental concept, and it should be front of mind in your quest to create a Lean business. It is what you should always be striving for: the day when the customer's orders tell you what to build, with very little intervention. At Wiremold, we had printers all over the shop floor that would print production *kanban* at the cell as customer orders came in throughout the day. This allowed us to connect the customer directly to the production cell, thus cutting lead times and improving customer service. It also connected our workforce to the customer, which was great for morale. We needed production planning only for our seasonal buildup. Other than that, it was sell one, make one with the customer calling the shots on the shop floor.

In addition, pull should not be restricted just to your customers. It should be used throughout the value chain. It is particularly helpful in tying you to your suppliers. If you want to be Lean and responsive to your customers, you have to be in a position where you can make every product every day. You probably won't actually have to do this, as your customers won't order every product every day. Even so, you need to be capable of doing this without carrying a lot of raw material inventory. This means that you will have to rely on your suppliers.

My rule of thumb is that, at a minimum, vendors should deliver daily based on a simple *kanban* pull signal. Vendors will resist at first, but keep in mind that you are the customer. Frequent deliveries mean that the amount of raw material on hand will drop dramatically, as will the cost of carrying it. The space needed to store all that material will be freed up for more productive purposes, like growing the business. Your costs will go down. In addition, the labor used to move inventory around can be reduced or redeployed. The finance team will no longer have to track the excess. And once you get a vendor to deliver daily, the disruption of running out of stock on those parts is virtually eliminated.

For bulky parts or major raw materials needed for production, move to multiple deliveries per day as soon as possible. At Toyota, bulky parts like tires, seats, gas tanks, and the like can be delivered as frequently as 32 times per day, sequenced for what is being built and when. Smaller items, such as bolts and other fasteners, come two to four times per day. At Wiremold, we got six to eight truckloads of steel per day, despite the fact that our supplier was more than 300 miles away. We carried only one or two days' worth of raw steel compared with three to four months' worth before we started our Lean conversion.

One great pull system that I saw in Japan was at Horie Metals, which made gas tanks for Toyota. In the final assembly area of the plant, the company had a printer spitting out orders from Toyota at set intervals indicating the next four gas tanks that were needed. The plant knew approximately how many gas tanks Toyota needed each day, but Horie made many versions of its gas tanks, and it never knew what models would be ordered, and in what sequence, until the information was printed. Each gas tank was then built and loaded onto a special trailer parked at the end of final assembly. Every 45 minutes or so, the trailer would take off for Toyota and be replaced by the next trailer.

The trailers arrived at the Toyota assembly plant's gas-tank installation station, where robots did all the work. The conveyor line had a mixture of car models (reflecting what was being ordered by customers), and, just to complicate things a bit, not all of them got a gas tank. (Japanese taxis tend to use propane gas, and the tanks for this were installed at a different location.). I asked the plant manager when he was able to tell Horie what the next four gas tanks would be. He said he did not know until the cars came out of the paint operation and were on the assembly line—just about two hours before each car needed the gas tank installed.

The entire Toyota assembly plant had less than two hours of total gas-tank inventory. Horie only had one or two days of total inventory and no finished goods. This is only one small link in the very complicated pull system that Toyota uses, but it is a good illustration of how processes between two real-world customers are linked to create a pull system.

These fundamentals—pull, standard work, one-piece flow, and *takt* time—should be the lens through which you view your organization and any of the challenges you face. When you are stumped by a hard problem—like the time I was asked to lead a *kaizen* to help an emergency room at a local hospital that was overly burdened with psychiatric patients—go back and follow these four fundamentals to find the right solution. If you run into resistance in your organization, again, return to the fundamentals to help you lead people back to the right path. Lean fundamentals give you the framework to move the ball forward, always toward a more Lean organization. You will learn many more Lean tools along the way, but these four fundamentals are the foundation on which your Lean transformation will be built.

Where Is Lean Taking You?

Now it's time for you to start your Lean transformation. Before you start aggressively running kaizen events, however, you need to consider a few vital things. You need to articulate your strategy clearly and set the stretch goals that you will need if you are to get there. You should articulate the core values that you plan to use to guide your team on its Lean transformation. And you should obtain the expert Lean knowledge you will need to train all your people up front. Staffing your kaizen promotion office with outside Lean experts and engaging a top Lean consulting firm will get you in good shape here. Lastly, if you can, add Lean knowledge to your board as soon as possible. This will make the Lean work that follows a lot easier.

Now that you've learned the management musts and the four Lean fundamentals, it is time to start your Lean transformation. I believe that the first step is to establish a clear vision of what you are trying to achieve. You should think of this in business terms. You are not trying to become a Lean consultant. You are running a business, and you have an obligation to both your shareholders and your employees to do this as well as you can. So, let's think of this in two parts. Your first objective should be to use Lean as a strategic weapon to improve your value-adding activities and vastly improve your results. A good initial target would be for you to beat the Wiremold results shown in Chapter 1 (or, if you are a service company, something similar to these results). I am sure you can do this because at the time we sold Wiremold, all the members of my team felt that we were only scratching the surface of what was possible.

Your second reason to make the shift to Lean is the responsibility that you have to your people. I always felt that my biggest obligation was to the people in my organization. My first priority was to protect their jobs (a successful, growing company does this best), and after that, to provide opportunities for personal growth and wealth creation. Switching to a Lean strategy for my businesses always created the type of learning environment that allowed these things to happen. Of course, I can't force you to think the same way about this as I do. I can, however, tell you that the desired financial results will be a lot harder to achieve if you don't do the right things for your people.

Lean Strategy

Everything starts with your strategy. You'll need a strategy statement that articulates your vision and incorporates the stretch goals that are required to achieve it. The need to have your strategy statement brief, simple, and repeatable cannot be overstated. Even if your people don't fully understand where you are taking them, being able to repeat the words of your strategy will make all of them understand that they are all part of the same team, going in the same direction.

When creating your strategy, avoid saying anything that will limit your upside. Make your strategy broad enough and generic enough that your vision will fit any future acquisitions that you make. The fundamental transformation that you are undertaking is the removal of all the waste from your value-adding activities so that your business will be able to compete on its operational excellence. As a result, it is important that your strategy lay out the defining parameters of the operational excellence that you envision. Set your sights high.

In fact, set all your targets above the best-known results in your industry in order to best the competition in all categories. For example, a company with 3 inventory turns should adopt 20 inventory turns as an initial goal. A target of simply doubling the inventory turns makes people think that they just need to work a little bit faster. If the goal is 20 turns, it is clear that you need to rethink everything. If you are an insurance company that takes 40 days to respond to an application for insurance, then set your goal at 5 days, or if you are a hospital with an average wait time in the Emergency Room of 4 hours, set your target at 30 minutes. The important point here is that you should not fear stretch goals. There is a common misconception that people will become demoralized in the face of stretch goals and stop trying. However, experience has repeatedly proved to me that weak goals are what hold people back.

In preparation for my new job as CEO of the Wiremold Company, I wrote down my strategy for the company on a simple piece of paper. I then worked with my new staff to tweak it here and there. Together, we created a generic strategy that—aside from a few wording changes here and there—remained in place for more than a decade and was able to be applied to every acquisition (21 in all) that we did. In fact, it was so generic that it would still fit any manufacturing company, and, with a few simple changes, could fit most nonmanufacturing companies as well. As a result, I would like to share it with you here as an example of what I am talking about.

Wiremold Strategy

Be the leading supplier in the industries we serve and one of the top 10 time-based competitors globally;

1. Constantly strengthen our base operations
   - 100 percent on-time customer service
   - 50 percent reduction in defects per year
   - 20 percent productivity gain each year
   - 20 inventory turns
   - Visual control and the 5S's
2. Double in size every three to five years
   - Pursue selective acquisitions
   - Use QFD to introduce new products every month

The first part of this strategy statement (the vision) is fairly straight-forward. When I was at GE, Jack Welch was successful with a similar strategy: "Be number one or number two in all of our markets globally." The part about being a top time-based competitor is perhaps a little harder to grasp, as companies don't generally report things in terms of time (how long to enter an order, how long to change over a machine, how long from order to shipment, and so on). Even so, we recognized that it was important to keep shooting to be one of the best. For us to compete on time, we had to build operational excellence everywhere by improving all our processes. To define the operational excellence we were seeking, we used the targets listed in the tactical part of our strategy under the first point, "constantly strengthen our base operations." They are all stretch targets, to be sure. We believed that achieving these targets would allow us to reach our strategic goals of leadership in our market segments and being a top 10 time-based competitor. As a result, we effectively ran the company by focusing our attention on these five targets.

Because we understood that we would free up a lot of resources as we achieved these targets, we needed to add a growth element to the strategy in order to absorb them. This is Section 2, "double in size every three to five years." We started QFD[1] (quality function deployment) simultaneously with our *kaizen* process and cut our new product development times by 50 to 75 percent. This not only contributed to our growth, but generated additional cash that could be used for acquisitions. Our acquisitions occurred randomly, so all we could do there was be ready when the opportunity arose. Oh, and for those of you who want to know how this growth part of our strategy worked out, we doubled in size the first time in four years and then doubled in size again four years later. With a target of doubling every three to five years, I would say we were right on track.

Your strategy may be slightly different from this. That is fine. I used the Wiremold strategy as an example only because it worked very well. The key is to understand that you will need to define not only your vision, but also the operational improvements that you are targeting to make this happen. So, before you run out and start doing *kaizen* projects, make sure that your vision is translated into a clear, simple strategy that is easy for your people to understand and follow.

Articulate Core Values

Right after you develop your strategy, I suggest that you articulate your company's core values. A Lean organization requires teamwork, trust, and respect for people, so being able to articulate your core values at the same time as (or shortly after) you announce your Lean strategy will be very beneficial. After all, your company will reach its goals only if everyone is rowing together. Think of your core values as the guideposts that will guide your workforce toward your ultimate goal of having a Lean culture in your company.

The core values should be the few key things that are most important to your organization—not a laundry list. They should be simple and lasting. Remember, a company cannot change its core values every few years without losing the respect and confidence of its people. For guidance, the three core values we used at Wiremold are given here. In addition, Figure 4.1 shows the symbol that we displayed to remind everyone of these values. We included this symbol on all of our internal communications. The Q in the middle stands for quality. It is there to remind people that if we are true to our core values, quality would shine through in every thing we did.

Wiremold Core Values

People

Customers

Kaizen

Figure 4.1 Wiremold Core Values Symbol

Our first interest was always the people. For management, putting people first on our list of core values was a constant reminder that we wanted to attract, retain, and train the best possible people, and to give everyone avenues to grow. Naturally, the way we treated our people was our primary concern. We tried to create an atmosphere in which it was acceptable—even desirable—to fail. Failure, we said, meant that you were trying something new. In fact, I used to get mad at some of our engineers and managers and tell them that they weren't failing enough. I told them that progress came faster when you learned from your mistakes. Having no failures meant that either we weren't trying hard enough or we were saving up for that one big failure that could really harm the whole company. They thought this was a little strange at first, but once they understood that no one was going to get mad at them for trying something new, they relaxed and made a lot of progress.

Everyone participated on *kaizen* teams, and we tried to maintain an atmosphere of constant learning. We spent a lot of time and energy on our people. About one-third of my time was spent mentoring, training, and encouraging associates, as well as conducting group meetings discussing job satisfaction, benefits, and the company's direction.

The link between our people and our customers in our core values was *kaizen*. Being on a *kaizen* team meant, first, becoming more closely connected to customer needs and demands. *Kaizen* work also addressed customer problems. So, the entire improvement initiative was about getting closer to our customers and delivering value and operational excellence that our competitors could not match.

The core values that you write may be completely different. The important thing is to develop your list, present it to your employees, and take concrete actions to support each value. At Wiremold, we made a commitment to get every employee on a *kaizen* team within 9 to 12 months. The same was true at Jacobs Chuck and Jake Brake. In several of my portfolio companies, we addressed customer problems with *kaizen* teams that included a heavy dose of senior management. At Wiremold, we did an annual employee survey, and then the vice president of human resources and I met with every team for an hour of follow-up discussion based on the results of the survey that was designed to unearth issues that might not come up in daily operations.

Obtain the Lean Knowledge

In addition to developing your Lean strategy and core values, one of the most critical issues you have to solve before you start is where you will get the in-depth Lean knowledge that you will need if you are to drive the conversion and keep it on track.

For example, I would suggest that you, as the CEO, visit a few other companies that are well down the path of their own transformation. Talk with their CEOs and management teams. Find out what worked for them and what didn't. Go and participate on a few of their *kaizen* teams so that you get a firsthand feel for how they go about *kaizen* and what kind of results you can expect from a one-week *kaizen*. Perhaps you can even talk them into running a few *kaizen* events in one of your facilities. If so, make sure you are on the team. This will give you a good sense of how much opportunity exists in your company and allow you to see how your people react. These things will help, but they certainly won't make you a Lean expert by any means. As a result, you still need to get access to the proper Lean expertise if you are going to be successful.

My suggestion would be to go down two paths at the same time:

- Create a *kaizen* promotion office staffed with Lean experts.
- Add some Lean consulting help.

Back when I started my Lean journey, we couldn't really go out and hire Lean expertise, as there just wasn't any available. We had to train our own, which you also need to be doing as you move along. However, you now have the option of hiring excellent Lean expertise from the outside, and you should take advantage of this. In our portfolio companies, we use this dual-path approach plus a strong push on Lean from the board, and it works very well.

Start by hiring someone with proven Lean skills (i.e., someone who is well-versed in the Toyota approach to *kaizen* and comes from a company with a very strong reputation for what it has done in converting to Lean) as head of your new *kaizen* promotion office. This should be a high-level position; you might even want to have it report to you. This individual can then bring in other Lean experts to build his staff or can simply train your existing people (or some combination of the two). Make sure that your future "stars" get this training early and spend a couple of years working in the *kaizen* promotion office. As you go forward, having a strong Lean foundation should become a key element in who gets promoted to the next level. In parallel with this internal effort, you should also be trying to bring in the best possible outside expertise.

Hire a Lean Consultant

I am certainly not a fan of traditional consulting companies. They take your own data, massage them, and then spit them back to you in a fancy PowerPoint presentation, all the while charging you *way* too much money. But don't worry, I'm not suggesting that. Lean consultants don't work that way.

Lean consultants are more hands-on trainers than traditional consultants. They will roll up their sleeves and work with your *kaizen* teams to make real changes in your operation. So don't let the word *consultant* throw you. Lean experts will help you (and, more important, your people) see the waste, and then show you how to remove it.

Most good Lean consultants can trace their lineage back to Toyota, and, in many ways, Lean consultants in the United States are the descendants of the originals: Shingijutsu Consulting. These godfathers of the Lean movement all worked at Toyota with Taiichi Ohno and left Toyota to spread Lean around the globe with Ohno's blessing and encouragement. I had the honor and the singular experience of being their first U.S. client while I was working as a group executive at Danaher Corporation.

Our first day with Shingijutsu (and, by the way, their first day consulting in the United States) was at Jacobs Chuck in Clemson, South Carolina, in August 1987. Dennis Claramont, the president of Jacobs Chuck, and I hired Japanese interpreters from Clemson University and set up what we thought was an ambitious agenda. We set aside the morning for introductions, an overview of the drill chuck line, and a plant tour. Ten seconds into our 45-minute overview of the drill chuck, one of the consultants waved his hand dismissively and said, "We have those in Japan too. What's next?"

The scheduled 90-minute plant tour ended 80 yards into the plant. Total time: 2 minutes. We were already more than two hours ahead of schedule. The Shingijutsu consultants pointed us back to the conference room, where their president, Yoshiki Iwata (an original member of the Toyota Autonomous Study Group), went to the whiteboard and wrote, "No good." Turning back to the group, he said, "Look, everything here is no good. What do you want to do about it?"

Dennis said that his biggest problems were in heavy-duty industrial chucks. Iwata said, "Fine. Nakao and Takenaka will work on that, and I will work on assembly." So we formed two teams. Dennis and I stayed with Iwata, and a team of six or eight managers and engineers went with Chihiro Nakao and Akira Takenaka.

Two hours later, we were in the conference room and Iwata was telling us how to change the assembly lines. He was saying, "Get rid of all the conveyers. I hate conveyers," when two guys from the other team came in and cornered Dennis. They looked upset. After they left, I asked Dennis what they wanted. He said that Nakao and Takenaka wanted to move eight large machines over lunch. These machines had not been moved since their installation, 15 or 20 years earlier, so the team was nervous about it. To his credit, Dennis told them to go ahead and move the machines. After lunch, we went out and watched this. Two consultants, who had showed up that day in suits and ties (it was almost 100 degrees in the plant), were using pry bars and helping fork-lift drivers move the equipment. The people on Dennis's team were standing there with their mouths open. I thought, wow, these are my kind of consultants!

Shingijutsu set up the first cell for Jacobs Chuck that day. Even though we did not have time to get it all hooked up, Nakao showed us how the product should flow. With this as a start, and with a lot more quality time with Shingijutsu, Jacobs Chuck eventually tripled in size and went from breaking even to making a 20 percent pretax profit. This was a great result, but it took time. The first cell was a bit of a nightmare. The machines kept breaking down or going out of tolerance.

When one went down, the whole line stopped. This, of course, was by design, but it certainly didn't make things any easier. Dennis and his team never wavered. They stuck with it, fixed the problems one at a time, and got the great results.

The consultants from Shingijutsu never wrote a report or made a PowerPoint presentation. They were hands-on teachers in our offices and on our shop floors—just as every good Lean consultant has been since that time. They introduced us to the paperwork that Toyota used to run *kaizen* events and showed us how to organize and run a *kaizen*. They were tough on us (they referred to themselves as "insultants," not consultants), but we learned that there were no shortcuts. Their approach was to learn by doing. This is very effective, and it is how you and all your people should expect to learn as well.

When you engage a Lean consultant, make sure that he/she knows your values and your strategy, and that he adheres as closely as possible to the Toyota approach to *kaizen*. Meet frequently to ensure that the consultant stays aligned with your trajectory. And be prepared to work with that consultant for years, as opposed to on a project-by-project basis. Oh, and by the way, any Lean consultant that is worth hiring knows that he/she can't get results unless the CEO is fully committed and driving the change. If the Lean consultant senses you are not, don't be surprised if he/she comes in one day and fires you as a client. Even in the area of consultants, Lean is 180 degrees different from the traditional approach.

To give you some idea of how much consulting time you will need, my rule of thumb would be that if you have between two and five factories, you should commit to at least one consulting week per month for the first three to five years. The typical *kaizen* lasts one week, and a good consultant can mentor three or four teams each week. So, you can run 36 to 48 consultant-led *kaizen* events per year, and if you put 10 people on a team, 360 to 480 of your people can work directly with a Lean expert during the first year. This is how you leverage outside consultants. Combine this with *kaizen* projects led by your own internal experts from your *kaizen* promotion office and Lean will spread farther, faster.

The most common mistake I see companies make is hiring a Lean consultant and letting the consultant run six or eight *kaizen* events, but then saying, "Gee, we get the hang of this now." Then the consultant is fired, and before you know it, the company's Lean efforts have rolled backward or stopped because nobody knew how to sustain the improvements or how to move forward. How long you continue to use external Lean experts is, of course, up to you. We were still using them at Wiremold after 10 years, although we did cut back a bit in the later years. You probably should think in terms of three to five years starting out. Remember, Lean principles are easy, but implementing them and sustaining the gains are not. Get some help before you start your Lean transformation.

In the appendix, I have suggested several Lean consultancies and also recommended some key Lean resources for your consideration.

Add Some Lean Expertise to the Board of Directors

I've learned that it is important to add some Lean expertise to your board before you start your *kaizen* activities. This isn't as critical as the things we have just discussed, and in fact it can be done even after you start you transformation. But remember that making the switch to Lean is hard work. It will be even more difficult if your board either does not understand or disapproves of your direction. Having seen this unfold at more than one company, when I arrived at Wiremold, I moved quickly to add John Cosentino to the board of directors. As the other group executive at Danaher, John had worked with me on implementing Lean and was a powerful advocate of Lean, helping the other board members understand its importance. Existing board member Joe Day, who was also the CEO of Freudenberg-NOK, became convinced and began his own very successful Lean transformation at the billion-dollar elastomeric technology giant. Before long, then, I had two Lean advocates on the board, and I was convinced that the right board can make a big difference.

A great example is a former J. W. Childs Associates portfolio company, American Safety Razor (ASR). When I joined the board, this was a traditional company with no interest in Lean. Naturally, I was convinced that we could change the company's fortunes with a Lean path. I had the backing of three other directors, who were also partners at J. W. Childs, and I was able to get a strong Lean thinker, Don Beaver, into the position of vice president of operations. This laser-sharp focus on Lean from the board of directors, plus a lot of hard work from the people at ASR, overcame management's reluctance and produced the following results in Table 4.1 over about a three-year period.

Table 4.1   Lean Led from the Board: American Safety Razor

Item	Result	Percent Change
Inventory turns	2.5 times to 6.2 times	+148%
Working capital as % of sales	34% to 15%	− 50%
Customer service	85% to 98%	+ 15%
EBITDA margin	17% to 23%	+ 35%
Cash freed up from working capital	$65 million	n.a.

When J. W. Childs sold the company, we realized three and a half times our investment. Without the constant push toward Lean from the board of directors, none of this would have happened. So think about getting some Lean expertise on your board early in your transformation.

Now that you know where you want to go with Lean, know how you will get there, and have added some Lean knowledge to the company, it's time to see what happens on the ground as you get the work going.

Reorganize Your People Around Value Streams

You can't just drop Lean on a traditional (batch) organizational structure and hope to be successful—you will need to make a fundamental change to a value-stream type of structure. As you start your Lean work, determine the new roles (value-stream leader or team leader, for example), consider whom you want to put in these roles, and then announce this to your organization before you begin your first serious kaizen efforts. It doesn't have to be up and functioning the next day. The important thing is that the organization knows what's coming. Also consider a reduction in workforce before you begin your kaizen efforts (which will help with your guarantee of no job losses as a result of kaizen).

The biggest, and most common, mistake that I see companies make is thinking that they can somehow move to a Lean strategy while preserving a traditional organizational structure. This can happen only if you are okay with pretending to be Lean. If you want to truly *be* Lean and get all the benefits available from this, you can't maintain your traditional structure.

Let me give you some examples. Lean strategy calls for making products (or providing services, as the case may be) in a one-piece flow, as this provides the best quality, lowest cost, and fastest response to the customer. Your current structure, however, has functional departments based on equipment type if you are a manufacturer, or based on some narrow skill set if you are a service company. The only way to change to one-piece flow is to bust up the functional silos. In addition, the move to Lean requires a *pull* system where you can connect the customer demand directly to the shop floor, thus drastically cutting lead times. The traditional approach, on the other hand, uses a material resource planning (MRP[1]) system and a forecasting system to *push* production through to the shelf in the hope that someone will buy it. This is true for distributors and retailers as well as for manufacturing companies. Service companies don't necessarily use MRP, but they often have some sort of batch process (like entering everything into the computer) that takes place before they release their incoming demand to the first functional silo. Push systems and pull systems are exactly opposite. In addition, in the traditional organization, the way we sell things, develop new products, and even do the accounting are all almost exactly opposite from the way we want to do the same things with Lean.

This notion that "everything has to change" is a big hurdle for most CEOs to get over. It's one of the reasons that so few organizations have made the Lean transformation. At the heart of a Lean turnaround, you are really trying to transform your people. Lean requires that people change their thinking, including their most basic instincts about how to organize work. The more seniority and status a person has, the harder he will be to change. You can't just one day say, "OK, everyone: now you have to change the way you think about how work is done" and have it happen. This approach will go nowhere. You have to lead the change.

Here's a powerful idea for making this happen: recognize that switching to Lean requires both the organization and the people to change. You can use one as a lever for the other. In other words, to change the people, change their environment. Remind yourself that structure drives behavior. So, get your people out of their silos as quickly as possible. I recommend doing this before the first *kaizen* (we did it that way at Wiremold, and it worked very well). Even if the restructuring is only on paper at first, make sure that everyone knows what is coming so that there are no surprises.

The Value-Stream Organization

The value-stream organization structure that I am describing here is focused on the way you structure your value-adding activities. Your traditional structure at the top (e.g., vice presidents of sales, marketing, engineering, human resources, operations, finance, and information technology) can largely stay the same, although the approach has to change (as we will discuss later in this chapter). Below this level, however, you should flatten out the organization so that the new value-stream leaders report frequently to the CEO and the senior team as if they were one "senior management team." At Wiremold, for example, most of the value-stream leaders reported directly to the VP of operations but had a strong dotted-line reporting relationship with the senior management team. Because most of your people are in value-adding roles, this organizational change will affect the bulk of your people.

What I am talking about here is getting rid of all functional departments and creating new teams based on value streams (or product families). All companies, whether manufacturing or service, have clearly identifiable value streams (product families) that can be grouped together and headed by a team leader. At Wiremold (before Lean), we split our financial reporting into six product families, even though they were made physically in functional departments. In a life insurance company, the process of getting an application for a new policy all the way through to the issuing of that policy to the customer is a value stream. In most life insurance companies, however, the actual work is done by various functional departments (data entry, case management, underwriting, policy issuance, and so on) that are not linked.

In a value-stream organization, the team leader is given all the equipment needed to make the complete product as well as all the people—from operators to managers and engineers—and has designated support from the rest of the organization. You don't need to buy additional equipment to do this. Just distribute the existing equipment among the new team leaders. When you run into a situation where

TEAM LEADER			
Buyer-Planner*	**Shop Floor**	**Engineering**	**Support****
	Manager	Industrial	Finance
	Cell Leaders	Manufacturing	HR
	Operators		Marketing
			IT

* The buyer-planner is an individual who procures material from vendors and does all production planning required by the team.

** A designated representative of each support function reports (dotted-line) to the value-stream team leader and attends all team meetings.

Figure 5.1 Value-stream Organization Chart

three teams use one piece of equipment, then give that equipment to the team leader who uses the most parts from it and let him supply the other two team leaders.

Because Lean allows you to connect the customer directly to the individual cells in each value stream, everyone on the team feels the pull of the customer directly. The team leader, in fact, is responsible for the customer service measurement for his value stream, further tying your people to the customer. This is vastly different from the traditional structure, where the bulk of your people have no customer exposure and their focal point is just your internal forecast: "make the forecast."

Figure 5.1 shows a typical value-stream structure[2] with a team leader and all of his staff.

The Team Leader

The team leaders for product families or value streams are critical positions in a Lean organization. In a flow environment, there are no functional leaders, such as stamping or drilling (or, if you are an insurance company, case management or underwriting). Also, you will not need centralized purchasing, production planning, or shop-floor engineering. Instead of being centralized, these functions should be split up and the people assigned to product family or value-stream teams, under the direction of the team leader. For example, the buyer-planner role at Wiremold was a single individual who was responsible for production planning, product releases from the vendors, and some purchasing for the items that were unique to his team. This change (plus a drastic reduction in the number of raw material vendors) allowed us to eliminate both the planning and purchasing departments and gave us better results.

When you choose people for team leader roles, find those who can lead, and who are self-motivated problem solvers capable of running a small business. The value stream's team leader not only will have all the equipment necessary to make the complete product in one pass, but will own all of the key measurements for the group's products. That means that the team leader is ultimately responsible for reporting the products' customer service scores, productivity, quality, and inventory turns and the visual production environment. Team leaders also interface with inside and outside sales, and give weekly progress reports on the key measurements to the CEO and senior staff.

In effect, every team leader is running a reasonable-sized business. This requires people with broad capabilities—but not necessarily a manufacturing background—and should attract high-potential individuals. Four of the first eight team leaders at Wiremold had no manufacturing background, and only two of the eight had been functional department heads. In fact, two were women (one from inside sales and one from IT), one was from marketing, and another was from finance. All the team leaders had their offices out on the production floor in their team area. All but one adapted very well and did an excellent job. Only the marketing guy didn't make it. He was more than capable of doing the job, but he had an attitude problem, and he talked down to everyone on his team. When we were trying to promote teamwork and a new way of doing things, this just didn't work.

The CEO should be closely involved with this selection process, and should stay involved for the long term. (All of these team leaders should have the ability to rise in your organization over time.) That means having the CEO and senior staff available when team leaders report their results. At Wiremold, we did this every week, and I found that giving each team leader 10 minutes a week for reports was more than sufficient. What is critical here is constancy. Having all the key decision makers in the room allows you to respond quickly to any issues that the team leaders are experiencing. In this way, the senior management team is tied directly to the value-adding workforce and is making on-the-spot decisions to make the workers' jobs better (i.e., improve the value-adding activities).

Also, I strongly suggest that you select the value-stream leaders and move the organizational structure into place before the first *kaizen*. This way, there will be a leader in place to receive the benefits of that first *kaizen*, and also to be responsible for all follow-up tasks to ensure that the improvements are cemented in place. Even though their equipment will still be scattered around in the former functional layouts, the new team leaders can still take responsibility and get going.

The *Kaizen* Promotion Office

As part of this value-stream organization, you need to create and staff a support operation for the Lean transformation. This is often called a *kaizen* promotion office (KPO) or continuous improvement office (CI), and it is a critical function. The team leader of this office should be at least equal in stature to the value-stream team leaders. The office should be staffed with a few outside Lean experts plus people from throughout your organization that you have identified as change agents. The full-time job of the people in this office is to run and follow up on *kaizen* projects, and to train the rest of the organization in Lean principles and techniques. A good rule of thumb for the size of this office is that it should grow to be 2 or 3 percent of your hourly workforce. It is a great training ground for your future leaders. Think of rotating your high-potential people into the KPO for two years and then promoting them to a higher position where they can apply their Lean skills.

In the shop-floor column of Figure 5.1, showing the new organizational structure, note that operators report to cell leaders, who report to managers. At Wiremold, the cell leaders had a critically important role. All union members, these cell leaders made an extra dollar an hour to perform the role, and, because cell leaders had to be able to operate every machine in each multifunctional cell, the union agreed that leaders could be selected based on capability and not just seniority. Leaders often had three or four cells to manage; they handled all logistics and did problem solving in their cells, but did not have management authority.

Herding Cats

Reorganizing by value stream makes sense, but it is not as simple to do as I described. The reason, of course, is the resistance that you can expect from your people. They haven't had any *kaizen* experience, so this will all seem strange to them. "This will never work." "You can't put a nonmanufacturing person on the shop floor." "No one else knows how to do this job" (the refrain in most service companies). "Shop floor engineers need to sit with other engineers, not in some production team." "You can't just not have a planning department or a purchasing department." These are just a few of the things you should expect to hear. Getting all your people on the same page will be like herding cats, but in making the Lean transformation, that's one of your new roles: "cat herder in chief."

One of your most important duties in your herding role is to get your senior management team on board. This won't be easy. Your senior managers are all used to running their own fiefdoms. So if a member of senior management fights the Lean approach at every turn—and this does happen—it is your responsibility to either convince that person to get on board or let him go. My advice is to give naysayers a chance, but do not give them too long to get on board. Some people simply cannot change and will not be able to see past their most obvious interest, which is protecting their existing fiefdom.

If you do acquiesce and allow one senior person to remain the unchanged ruler of his own kingdom, you might have a situation similar to one that I faced at Carrier Corporation, circa 1991. I had agreed to help a friend (Carrier's CEO) introduce Lean to the big air-conditioning company. Carrier was a worldwide company with control of North American operations mostly centralized in Syracuse, New York. The human resources (HR) department, in particular, was adamant about running everything related to people in every U.S. plant through Syracuse. All the Carrier plants were large and employed many people, but the plant managers were not allowed to communicate directly with the workforce—that had to come from the HR wizards in Syracuse.

Before we began our first *kaizen*, I insisted that the vice president of operations give employees a no-layoff guarantee. The vice president, who was in charge of several Carrier plants, worried about skirting the centralized authority of HR in Syracuse, but he saw the need and so made his promise to the workforce. At our first *kaizen* event, in Collierville, Tennessee, we freed nearly 40 people from the project area, and in no time, word of the no-layoff promise blazed through Syracuse.

A couple of weeks later, we were preparing for a second *kaizen* week, this time in Knoxville, Tennessee, when HR sent a message expressly forbidding a no-layoff guarantee. The second in command from Syracuse's HR department came to Knoxville, bearing this message. This was August in Tennessee, and we were sweating on the shop floor in blue jeans, but this guy showed up every day in a suit, suspenders, and a bow tie, always trying to explain to me how important it was that Syracuse—and Syracuse alone—make any decisions regarding layoffs. By Wednesday of that week, it was clear that we could free up about 35 people from the process, and I needed to know what we would tell these folks on Friday. He said it would take corporate some time to make a decision.

"This *kaizen* ends in two days, and we need to redeploy 35 people," I said. "When can you decide?"

"I think we should be able to have an answer by November," he said. He left without giving a no-layoff-due-to-*kaizen* guarantee, but at least he did not force a layoff. He just put the whole effort in Knoxville into a temporary drift.

This was a classic example of fiefdoms created by silos. Our bow-tied friend would have done anything to retain power for his department—even harm the company's larger goals. It is my (fairly well-informed) guess that nobody had made a serious effort to convert this gentleman or his boss to Lean thinking prior to this *kaizen*. So he had no reason to diverge from his department's agenda.

Even with a value-stream structure in place, you have to be careful not to make other organizational mistakes. People are complicated, and they can be completely attached to methods of working, even if those methods are terrible and are hard on their own bodies and pocketbooks.

For instance, when I first met the European leadership team of one of my J. W. Childs portfolio companies, I could feel that there was tension in the group. The company had just been purchased by J. W. Childs Associates L.P., where I am a partner, and I became its new chairman. This was a $1.1 billon international company, with the biggest piece being in Europe. The company had been struggling for some time. One reason was that the prior management had organized it into two warring factions. The manufacturing plants, engineering, warehouses, and administrative functions were called Supply Chain and were treated as a cost center. The other part, called Sales & Marketing, was considered the money-maker. Each had its own profit and loss (P&L) and its own incentive targets. This caused excessive, continuous bickering between the two sides, with little focus on the customer. That distrust was evident in the mountain of inventory the company had built up between the two sides.

Following the standard Lean game plan, we reorganized the company into product families (value streams). We emphasized that it was products, delivered without waste and infighting, that make money. In addition, we converted to a single organizational structure and put everyone on the same bonus plan, with a common set of objectives. They had to work as one team, focused on the customer and not on each other. A few years later, when we had cut the company's $150 million European inventory down to $25 million, we might have looked like heroes or magicians. But really, all we were doing was addressing an entrenched organizational problem by restructuring the company and moving everyone's focus to implementing Lean and responding to the customer.

Do not underestimate the internal pressure within a group to keep doing and seeing things the same way as always. Even if the people on your staff tell you that they love your ideas and are completely on board, keep an eye out for unintentional backsliding. The biggest resistance to change will always come from senior and middle management; expect it and be prepared.

Consider a Reduction in Workforce Prior to Your First *Kaizen*

The next step I think you should take before starting your *kaizen* activity is to consider a reduction in workforce. To run a successful *kaizen* program, you must guarantee that there will be no layoffs as a result of *kaizen*. Yet, you are probably 25 to 40 percent overstaffed right now. Most companies are. If this can be a voluntary reduction, so much the better.

At Wiremold, we were fortunate to have an overfunded pension plan. We used these excess funds as a sweetener and achieved a 30 percent reduction in the workforce through an early retirement program. Our long-service employees, by the way, were very happy about this. To help cushion the sudden drop, we negotiated with the union to add a layer of temporary workers that would be capped at 15 percent of our workforce. This helped us guarantee the jobs of our permanent workforce. The temporary force also proved an excellent pool for us to draw on when filling permanent jobs. Try to make this happen before you start aggressive *kaizen* activity.

Go to the *Gemba* to Run Your *Kaizen*

Once you start your kaizen activity, you want to be able to go full speed ahead. When you announce your new Lean strategy to everybody, make sure that you are clear about why you are doing this and what type of results you expect. Don't send a memo. Your people need to hear this from you in person. Follow up your announcement with the initial training, and then start your kaizen activities. Try to go at a pace that averages two kaizen events per week per facility. As CEO, you should be involved in picking the areas for each kaizen (starting with your biggest product family first) and setting the stretch goals for the kaizen teams. Be prepared to move everything multiple times (this is true for both manufacturing and service companies) and to go back and run multiple kaizen events in the same areas. Your initial focus should be on eliminating batching and creating flow. Once you have flow (including standard work and working to takt time), you can create a pull system that connects your customers to the value-adding activities. This will allow you to compete on time and gain market share. The closer you get to the Lean ideal of "sell one—make one," the better off you will be. For service companies, think of "finish one before starting the next one."

Now that we have discussed most of the preparatory work that you need to do, it's time to go to the *gemba* and get started.

In Japanese, the word *gemba* does not mean just a shop floor or a work area. The *gemba* is the place in a company where value is created. In a hospital, where the customer values personal care above all else, the *gemba* is in surgical suites and at every patient's bedside. In farming, the *gemba* is the growing fields. In a factory, the *gemba* is the shop floor. If you have not been in the habit of spending time there, I strongly recommend that you get acquainted with it. Lean executives spend a lot of time in the *gemba*. How else could they know what the company needs?

Before we go there, however, I want to give you a little overview of how we will cover this. Applying Lean tools in order to get larger goals accomplished can lead to your getting buried in details. There are many Lean tools to use, such as SMED, TPM, 5S, and visual controls. In fact, many books have been written about each of these tools. But this is a business/management book aimed at helping you turn your company around using a Lean strategy, so we are not going to take a deep dive into the tools here. Instead, I want to focus on the things that I think I need to do, or at least be aware of, in order to lead your Lean transformation.

To set the stage, so to speak, let me remind you of the enormousness of the changes you are about to make. You are trying to shift your focus to improving your value-adding activities so that you can compete on your operational excellence and be a leading time-based competitor. To achieve this, you have to remove all the waste so that all your processes can improve. Because most companies, manufacturing and nonmanufacturing alike, produce things in batches, which hide the waste, we want to move to flow production, which exposes the waste.

Announcement and Initial Training

So where do we begin? I've already said that in order to switch to a Lean strategy, everything must change. That, plus the dramatic stretch goals of your Lean strategy statement, may seem traumatic to your organization. So make sure that you kick off your program in person (if your organization is too big, make a video so that everyone hears it from you directly). You need to make this as clear and simple as possible. You have to explain *why* you are doing this and *what* you expect to get as a result. You especially need to explain why it will be good for everyone.

Announcing the program will, of course, put you in front of all your people, saying that you are making a major change in direction and that you expect them to hit targets that your company has never even come close to in the past. You can expect that many of them will think that you've lost your mind: "This will never work here." "We can never reach those targets." To counter this, you need to appear confident—even if you have your own doubts. Cite examples of what other companies have achieved and why you are convinced that your company can get there, too. Present simple things that everyone can relate to. At Wiremold, I used a slide that just said:

Productivity = Wealth

I used this to drive home the rationale for the change and to help people understand that they would share in the wealth that was created. It also allowed me to build a sense of teamwork by explaining that we were going on this journey together, and that we would win only if everyone on the team contributed.

Your announcement of the Lean strategy needs to be followed quickly by initial training sessions that describe the Lean approach. While your Lean consultant and your *kaizen* promotion office (KPO) leader can help you put this together, I firmly believe that the CEO or a local leader—the division vice president, for instance—needs to deliver the training personally. Do not just introduce your Lean consultants and let them do it. Your people need to hear the details from you. This will help them understand that everyone will participate going forward, and that there is no opting out.

The initial training group should include, at a minimum, your senior managers and the union leadership if you have a union. Beyond that, you should include regional sales managers, plant managers, and other selected individuals from both the office and the shop floor. Target your natural leaders for the first training classes, since they are best suited to spread the word.

At Wiremold, our first training class consisted of 150 associates split into two groups. I put together the training manual and conducted a $1\frac{1}{2}$-day training session for each group, describing Lean principles and tools and laying out my expectations, such as going from 3 to 20 inventory turns. They were alarmed at the expectations, but I was there to tell them that it could and would be done. The key takeaway for them was that I was serious and committed, and that everyone had better get on board.

Now you are about to take your first handpicked teams out to the *gemba* and start to transform not just your own processes, but everyone's idea of what is possible. This is the fun part. So let's get started.

Pick the First *Kaizen* Projects

As CEO, you will need to know enough about operations to pick the first *kaizen* projects. Focus on areas where improvement will have the largest financial impact on your business. Do not go cautiously and slowly here; choose projects that will redesign and improve the biggest product or product family first. For subsequent projects, take the next biggest product family or focus on problematic areas such as operations that create bottlenecks. For machine-based manufacturing companies, a good rule of thumb is to do two setup *kaizen* projects each time, plus one that is focused on flow and one in the office. Non-manufacturing organizations might consider one *kaizen* project in support (i.e., office) functions for every two at the point of value creation. In any event, try to select the first several *kaizen* projects based on their ability to have a big-bang financial impact on the organization. Your KPO leader and Lean consultant can help you make the right choices.

If you delegate this chore of selecting the first *kaizen* projects to someone else, that person will most likely be fearful of creating big problems and will thus select targets conservatively, as I have witnessed many times. Nobody wants to make a mess, right? *Kaizen* projects on low-priority, tucked-away areas will have little effect, however, and will leave associates scratching their heads, wondering why you made a fuss about Lean.

Plan to be actively involved in *kaizen* selection throughout your tenure with the company. Not only will this signal your continued focus on improvement to everyone, but it will keep you connected to the organization's value creation. You can get input from your KPO, your vice president of operations, and the team leaders about what to tackle next. Make a list of their suggestions; then go to your shop floor with them and have a look. Make your final selections based on what you see there. The right choices should be very evident.

Stretch Goals

Work with the members of your senior staff and your Lean consultant to set stretch goals for every *kaizen*, and make sure that everyone knows about your personal involvement in creating the targets. It is critical that everyone knows that you think that your workers—using Lean principles—are capable of incredible achievements. Setting stretch goals is a compliment to your people—a sign of respect.

Do not be surprised, however, if your direct reports argue passionately for weaker, incremental goals. You may even be presented with a beautifully articulated list of "40 Reasons Why This Will Not Work." If you have done your homework and made contact with other Lean companies, you should be able to counter people's fears with a list of typical results from a one-week *kaizen*, documented by another company. Use the generic list given here (from my experience over many years), or obtain results from one of the Lean companies in your area that you have befriended.

Typical Results from a One-Week *Kaizen*

- Cut lead time 90 percent.
- Reduce staffing from 10 to 5.
- Reduce inventory by 70 percent.
- Reduce floor space by 50 percent.
- Reduce defects by 60 percent.
- Reduce travel distance by 90 percent.
- Cut setup time by 90 percent.

Running the *Kaizen*

Leading or being on a *kaizen* team yourself is the most personal, high-profile display of support that you can give the Lean transformation. Do not pass up this opportunity to earn respect and enthusiasm for the Lean effort. Be aware, however, that this is a time commitment, and that if you are leading a team, you have to be with that team the whole time. You can't be running back and forth to your office or be attached to your BlackBerry.

During a *kaizen* week, every person on the team should be completely separated from his regular job for the week. The team's undivided focus on a singular objective is what makes *kaizen* such a powerful tool. It is a doing exercise, not a planning exercise. If people attend meetings or take phone calls relating to their regular job during a *kaizen* week, you won't hit your targets. The CEO needs to model this focused behavior, especially as an example for senior staff members, and make improvement work the priority all week. Give the team enough time and support to ensure that all the *kaizen* goals are accomplished by week's end. Attendance on a *kaizen* team should be mandatory (like jury duty), and your support operations—such as maintenance and tool-rooms, or information technology if you are a service company—should give priority to requests from the *kaizen* teams when a *kaizen* is in progress.

Leading an improvement team means conducting the Monday morning *kaizen* kickoff, reviewing the situation in the target area, stating the goals for the week, maybe teaching a few simple tools, and then doing what you do best: leading people toward goals. It is good to have a Lean consultant on hand to fill in knowledge gaps, keep teams focused, challenge the old ways, and help teams maneuver around hurdles as they come up. As CEO, you should plan to participate on *kaizen* teams four to six times a year; there are few other ways to learn Lean and get a deep, firsthand knowledge of your company—the value added, the personalities, the problems, and the opportunities. Encourage the members of your staff to be on an equal number of *kaizen* teams every year.

Even when you are not scheduled to participate on a team, try to be available for the Monday kickoff sessions as often as possible. Less than an hour of your time will have a big impact. Also, attend as many of the daily team leader meetings as you can, and always go to the Friday final report meetings with all of your senior staff. Every organization with an ongoing Lean effort has built a culture around the Friday report meetings. They are a great way to celebrate the big gains that each team achieved during the week. The teams' results should also be published in the employee newsletter and posted on the bulletin boards so that those who are not on a *kaizen* team that week can also celebrate the improvements.

What to Expect

While you will see some amazing results immediately, it takes time for the Lean effect to hit most companies. As a rule of thumb, most companies will need to do Lean-focused *kaizen* work for three to five years before they are ready to even think about competing on operational excellence. In fact, my experience has been that it takes even a great team about four years before people finally can see how much opportunity still lies ahead. (Don't worry; you will be seeing significant gains along the way.) This is a critical period for the CEO, who must keep the Lean momentum going—even when others cannot yet see the results on P&L statements.

Of course, the more *kaizen* work you do, the faster your organization will progress. I recommend that you average two *kaizen* projects per week per facility. This pace will help you train as many people as quickly as possible, but there is a more practical reason as well. During your early first steps into Lean, you will be running a part batch and part flow operation, and you want to move away from these dueling systems as soon as possible. Once you have made your announcement and started your *kaizen* effort, it should be full speed ahead. You can't dabble at this and expect results.

You should focus your initial *kaizen* efforts on creating flow in a few selected areas to help speed the transition. Scattering *kaizen* efforts across the company so that a broad array of people and facilities get exposure might seem like a good idea, but this strategy tends to diffuse the Lean effect. Think about concentrating all your early work on creating a model product line or model factory to showcase the Lean organization that is being created. If you focus on creating a model factory, for instance, you could have your other plant managers participate in a *kaizen* activity at the model factory every month or every six weeks, then go home and implement something that they learned each time. This way, you get focused achievements from the model factory and still make progress elsewhere. If you are a hospital, you may select one of your major value streams, say anything related to the heart, as your "model factory." Or, if you are a service company, maybe select a regional office as the "model factory."

Be prepared to move all of your equipment (or rearrange your workstations if you are a service company) multiple times while working out the best way to create flow. Make sure you publicly support this. As long as you make improvements as a result of the new configuration, go ahead and move the equipment. Do not run a return on investment (ROI) report on it. At Wiremold, I was once asked for permission to knock a hole in a wall in order to make a very large rolling mill fit into the space designated for a new cell. This was early in our Lean journey, and around 8:30 p.m., the *kaizen* team members came up to me on the shop floor to tell me that the new cell, as envisioned, just would not work—not unless, they said, someone took out most of a wall. I just looked at the team members in front of me and said, "Go ahead and do it." It made their day. They had the hole cut the next day, and the cell worked great. At the end of the week, team members told me how wonderful it was to take action, as opposed to just talking about things that we might do in the future. I had a few new Lean converts.

We went back to that cell many times for future *kaizen* projects and improved it every time, despite the fact that the rolling mill was still sticking through the wall. Remember: returning to an area many times with *kaizen* projects is expected in a Lean world. This is a game of improvements, after all, not singular fixes. We want a culture of continuous improvement.

A Lean transformation can be described as a journey with two major movements: creating *flow*, and then creating *pull*. Your initial focus, as I mentioned earlier, should be on creating flow. And just like any momentous journey, having a checklist handy will help you make sure that your organization remains on track.

Checklist for Creating Flow—Manufacturing Companies

☐ Make safety the first priority.
☐ Reduce all setup times to less than 10 minutes.
☐ Reduce work-in-process (WIP) inventory to minimum levels (one piece per machine).
☐ Move all production equipment into working cells.
☐ Establish one-piece flow in all cells.
☐ Create and enforce standard work at every workstation.
☐ Establish water spiders where needed.
☐ Negotiate daily deliveries with all vendors.
☐ Reduce raw materials.
☐ Begin total productive maintenance (TPM).
☐ Inspect and repair all dies and molds after each use.

- ☐ Use 5S procedures to clean up and establish safe work areas.
- ☐ Paint all equipment as you go.
- ☐ Install brighter lighting.
- ☐ Reduce the size of production runs.
- ☐ Reduce finished goods inventory.

Checklist for Creating Flow—Nonmanufacturing Companies

- ☐ Make safety the first priority.
- ☐ Create a value-stream map to see the steps in the process.
- ☐ Rearrange work centers in the value-stream sequence.
- ☐ Put the entry to Step 2 as close as possible to the exit from Step 1 (just hand the paper to the next person).
- ☐ Eliminate waiting and transportation time between steps.
- ☐ Create and enforce standard work for each step.
- ☐ Establish visual controls—production control boards.
- ☐ Make sure all necessary forms and supplies are within reach.
- ☐ Establish a replenishment system for forms and supplies.
- ☐ Use 5S procedures to clean up and organize work areas.

This is a pretty fundamental list. We don't need to talk about every item on it, but I do want to offer advice on a few of them.

Total Productive Maintenance

Total productive maintenance (TPM) is a foundational methodology of the Toyota Production System, and there are entire libraries of articles and books about this disciplined approach to machine maintenance. The concept of TPM is to first identify and then religiously perform those daily or periodic maintenance tasks that will ensure that each piece of equipment runs when it is required. If yours is a machine-reliant business, TPM will be part of the vital heart of your efforts. With Lean, you can no longer accept any machine breakdowns. This also holds true for any equipment in service companies (computers, for example) or hospitals (x-ray equipment, lab equipment, and operating room equipment, for example).

The 5S

Another equally important tool for creating flow and maintaining your lean effort is 5S. This is another discipline (tool) on which volumes have been written. To keep it simple here, I will just give you a brief description of each of the five. In order to create the basic discipline required to implement Lean, you will first have to make 5S second nature for everyone in your organization. Remember, 5S is applied everywhere.

At Wiremold, we had a multifunctional (including both hourly and salaried employees) 5S team that did a detailed 5S inspection of every team every two weeks. This was done in both the factory and the office (my office included, unfortunately). We awarded the winning team a banner to hang over its area, as well as free coffee and doughnuts for a week. This didn't cost us much, but it worked very well. Using 5S is a great discipline for any type of business. Many hospitals have seen tremendous gains just from implementing 5S in their overcluttered work areas.

In any event, a brief description of each of the items in 5S (which comes from the fact that the original Japanese words all start with an S) is as follows:

1. *Seiri*, or sort; to throw away what is not needed
2. *Seiton*, or straighten; to create and maintain order
3. *Seiso*, or shine; to clean
4. *Seiketsu*, or standardize; to develop rules to maintain the first three S's
5. *Shitsuke*, or sustain; to maintain the discipline of the first four S's

Setup Reduction

Setup reduction is the core foundational level of Lean. Almost all companies do some form of setup or changeover. Hospitals, for example, have to change over the operating room after every surgery and the patient room after every patient discharge. Without fast setups, one-piece flow and customer pull systems are impossible. The good news is that setup reduction is both easy and inexpensive (contrary to the beliefs of most engineers). The table on page xvi shows some great examples of this point. As CEO, your takeaway from this table should be that setup reductions of 90 percent after a one-week *kaizen* are possible on many types of equipment. Don't let your people try to talk you into lower targets.

Setup reduction work, however, will involve more than quick changeovers on individual machines, so be prepared. A batch company that uses punch presses, for instance, will find that all its dies are of different heights. To get rapid setups systemwide, you need one or two common shut heights for all dies. Dies will have to be altered, and this will take time. Develop a plan for this work as part of your setup reduction efforts.

Very early in our *kaizen* efforts at Wiremold, I told the team that we needed to get all our punch press dies to a common shut height as soon as possible. The head of our maintenance and toolroom, John Jakabauskas, was flabbergasted by this directive. John had been around a long time and was a really great guy, but I apparently pushed him over the edge with this one. "But, Art, you don't understand; you just can't do this," he said. "Why not?" I asked. "Because we have 1,600 dies and it will take forever," he said. My response to that was, "Gee, that's a lot; you'd better get started right away, then." It took three years, but John, as always, did a great job, and it really helped us.

While your teams are addressing shut heights, they should also be solving die out-of-service issues. Most traditional companies are accustomed to waiting for the repair of broken dies. This kind of time-consuming, reactive system is unacceptable in Lean. Every die has to be available when you need it—no excuses. The same is true for equipment used in service companies. The computers have to run, x-ray machines have to work, and the planes have to fly—no excuses. To create a proactive environment, Wiremold set up a separate maintenance and repair toolroom right next to the main press area. Every die was opened and inspected after every run. Wiremold also created and maintained spare parts (no spare parts existed before Lean) for high-volume dies to enable fast repairs. Five or six toolmakers were inspecting and maintaining more than 500 dies per week. As part of TPM, teams created daily maintenance programs for the presses, as well. Operators were trained to run through a checklist of daily maintenance and inspection on every press, and the checklist was displayed at each station, with the operator's sign-off, so that the team leaders could easily see that the daily maintenance had been done. The same system can be used for the equipment used in service companies.

Creating One-Piece-Flow Cells

Move your machines into one-piece-flow cells (or, if you are a service business, line up the value-adding activities in such a way that a piece of paper gets handed from one so-called specialist to the next, never stopping or being put down until the work is complete). These cells will vary widely depending on the value stream. Some cells will make a few variations of a high-volume product; others may have groups of more versatile equipment that make two dozen different products in the value stream. When setting up these cells, follow the Lean principles discussed in Chapter 3. Put the equipment (or workstations if you are a service company) inside a cell close together to facilitate the operators' movements. Do not leave any room for WIP inventory except the standard one piece per machine (unless you have a drying or cooling requirement, in which case you may need more). For service companies, get rid of the in- and outboxes—this is your WIP.

Moving equipment into cells, eliminating WIP, and freeing up excess personnel to be assigned to other tasks will have a dramatic short-term impact. It is understandable to be excited, but do not be fooled. There will be no resting on any laurels. Extensive follow-up work will be required to make the new cells run correctly. You need to plan to run repeat *kaizen* events on one-piece-flow cells to cement the new work sequence in place and find new opportunities for improvement.

Free Up Floor Space

You should close the warehouses and rope off the space emptied by *kaizen* work. Do not allow anyone to stack WIP or other miscellaneous junk in the space you free up. In any company, empty space has an uncanny knack for filling up again. Because this space is your business's room to grow, it must be kept separate from today's operations. I have found that the best way to keep this space free until you need it is to put some form of simple employee recreation area there. At Jake Brake, we had a basketball court; at Wiremold, we had basketball, Ping-Pong, and a golf driving net. Employees won't dump pallets of material on their own basketball court. As a rule of thumb, a manufacturing company should expect to free up about half its floor space in 18 months to 2 years. Companies with low inventory turns will have even more space available quickly. The floor space gain for service companies will vary greatly but still should be in the 20 to 35 percent range.

Inventory Reduction

While every item on the checklist for creating flow is important, and all of them are integral to Lean, you will probably spend the most time and effort on inventory reduction. In fact, to my way of thinking, *inventory is the root of all evil.* For most companies, inventory reduction also provides the greatest benefit. This is true for hospitals, distributors, retailers, and many other service companies that have any type of traditional inventory. Banks, insurance companies, and similar organizations don't have much in the way of physical inventory, but they do have a lot of work in process in the form of "applications in process" that are tying up their space and their cash.

First, focus on reducing and then eliminating all that WIP. This will happen naturally as you move everything into one-piece-flow cells. Get as close as is possible to the ideal of one piece of WIP per machine. For office environments, think of one piece of paper on a desk at one time. Then, work on reducing raw material in parallel with creating flow. Get all of your vendors to deliver every day, using simple *kanban* cards or reusable boxes, when possible. Remember, inventory hides waste. In fact, I believe that inventory turns is the single most important Lean measurement. The company that turns its inventory 20 times annually will always deliver more value to customers at lower cost and higher quality than the company that turns its inventory 3 times annually.

Inventory reduction can be hard work for a lot of people. Try to have some fun along the way. One of my fondest memories of Wiremold, in fact, came from an inventory-reduction attempt at a new acquisition, Walker Systems, Inc. in Parkersburg, West Virginia, in 1994. This was a big, rambling old metalworking plant, and during one of the first *kaizen* weeks, I wandered over to the area where work-in-process inventory was stored. The company even had a name for it, the inventory control area, or ICA. With a pad of paper, Magic Marker, and some tape, I went to the first big rack of parts and put up a sign that said, "Parts Hotel Closing—This Rack Goes Away 2/25/94." I went down the line and put the same sign on every parts rack, with dates of elimination that were one month apart. I was walking away when I heard this voice say, "Hey, you, I need to talk to you."

The voice belonged to an attractive woman in a funny hat (she was known for her hats). She said, "What are you doing? My people are all upset." I asked if she was in charge of the inventory. She said that she was the manager of the ICA and that her name was Barbara Looney. I led her back to the "parts hotel."

"All of this inventory is waste," I said. "It's tying up our space and our cash, so I want you to eliminate one rack per month until they are all gone. Oh, and just to keep me up to speed, I want you to send me my sign each time a rack comes down."

A month later, I was in the plant for another *kaizen* and, on the day of final reports, Barbara came up to me and gave me the first sign, along with a poem she had written about the evils of inventory. Racks K&L were now gone, she announced in rhyme.

Ode to Art

"Inventory is evil," said King Arthur of *kaizen*.
So he came to Dame Barbie with his plan.
"You must make these horrid racks go away
Or February 25th is your banishment day."
Dame Barbie cried and wrung her hands,
But King Arthur had made his noble stand.
So she gathered her trusty knights around,
And now Racks K&L can't be found.

I thanked her and told her that she had done a great job, but she was not satisfied. "I gave you a poem, so I expect you to give me a poem back," she said. I am not a poet, but I dashed off a few quick stanzas. Then, just to play along, I read her poem and debuted my own effort, "The Parts Hotel," at the final *kaizen* presentation that week in front of about 60 people.

The Parts Hotel

Welcome to the parts hotel;
It's really quite the place!
We love our parts so very much
We give them lots of space.

They come on in to get a rest;
We treat them all the best.
They lay about for weeks or months
Just waiting to go out.

We love for them to gather dust;
In this we really trust.
And sometimes if we're lucky
They stay long enough to rust!

They have a lot of fun here.
They make a lot of buddies.
We feel we can sell them for more money
If they get a little cruddy.

The hotel is really spacious.
The racks go to the sky.
If we understood the waste here,
We'd all break down and cry.

> The parts fly in, but don't go out;
> They hope that they'll grow old.
> I'm sure you'll understand this;
> Their only other option is to finally get sold.
>
> They really like the staff here;
> They treat them with such care;
> Especially Dame Barbie
> And the hat that hides her hair.
>
> The location is also special;
> It's dark and out of the way.
> It's really pretty famous;
> They call it the ICA.
>
> But now the massive parts hotel
> With its racks up to the ceiling
> Has been exposed as massive waste
> And has that shrinking feeling.
>
> Dame Barbie has responded well
> The racks are coming down.
> Soon there will be no parts hotel
> And no extra parts doing nothing but lying around.

This impromptu poetry reading continued each month as more racks came down, and we always got a big laugh for our poetic efforts. (You can find all of these poems at http://mhprofessional.com/product .php?isbn=0071800670.) Even so, Barbara's work created significant improvement. In the end, we freed up 23,000 square feet of space and $2.6 million in inventory at Walker—a very good return on bad poetry.

The Path to Pull

Once you are well along the path of creating flow—meaning that you have established one-piece flow and standard work, and are working to *takt* time—the next step is to create pull across the value stream. This is not difficult conceptually, but it will take you some time and finesse. In a pull system, you are trying to respond to the demands of your customers as quickly as possible without creating any excess inventory (the biggest form of waste). This can best be done by using a simple card or signboard system—what I've previously defined as *kanban*. Done correctly, it is the link between you and your customers, allowing you to follow the Lean dictate of "sell one—make one."

As with flow, keeping a checklist handy for creating pull will help.

Checklist for Creating Pull—Manufacturing Companies

☐ Define the *kanban* quantity for each product.

☐ Generate *kanban* cards from all customer orders.

☐ Purchase raw material only with *kanban*.

☐ Use internal *kanban* to deliver parts where needed.

☐ Create supermarkets to buffer an uneven flow of parts.

☐ Establish a *heijunka* box to level the workload.

☐ Eliminate material resource planning (MRP) systems for scheduling the shop.

☐ Print *kanban* cards at the point of use.

☐ Have customers order by *kanban*.

☐ Reduce finished goods inventory.

Checklist for Creating Pull—Nonmanufacturing Companies

☐ For materials and supplies, follow the manufacturing checklist.

☐ Develop *kanban* cards for scheduling things like blood labs, MRI equipment, and operating rooms.

☐ For paper processing, set up one-piece flow and let that pull the paper forward.

☐ Use *kanban* cards to schedule customer visits or to move patients through a hospital until discharge.

Kanban

Creating a good, robust *kanban* system is not that easy. To begin with, it is the exact opposite of the MRP and forecasting method that you are probably using now. MRP is a high-inventory model, whereas *kanban* is a low-inventory model. As *kanban* are used to link the entire value stream together, it should not be surprising that there are different types of *kanban* cards for different links. (Customer *kanban*, conveyance *kanban*, production *kanban*, and vendor *kanban* are a few examples.)

You will need to determine how many *kanban* cards of each type should be in the system and what quantity of products or parts each *kanban* should represent. For high-volume products, each *kanban* card may represent a full pallet of material. For medium-volume products, a *kanban* card may represent a tote box containing 20 cartons of 10 each. For low-volume products, a *kanban* card could represent a single carton or even a single box. For custom products in a job-shop environment, you might need a *kanban* for each product, but you could have *kanban* for your standard component parts that equaled 10 or 20 parts. For a hospital, a *kanban* card could represent a patient and could be used to schedule services and track the patient until discharge.

Determining what a *kanban* quantity is and how many *kanban* you will need, however, is just the beginning. Next, you will have to teach your people how to handle the *kanban* cards so that they won't get lost. This was a big problem for us at Wiremold when we first got the system started. Next, you will have to deal with the demand fluctuations and seasonality of your sales pattern. As the volume of various products increases or decreases, the amount of *kanban* cards in the system will have to be adjusted. This needs to be done at least once per month.

Once you have sorted all this out, then the customer demand—either through your current system or by sending you a *kanban* card—initiates all the action. Let's say that you have six to eight factories, but you ship to customers through a centralized warehouse in order to satisfy their desire to receive different products on a single truck. In this case, the order will come into your system as it does now (perhaps to order entry or inside sales), and once it is entered, it will be printed in the warehouse to be shipped. Simultaneously, as orders come in throughout the day, *kanban* cards will be printed in the various production cells every time the order quantity reaches the level of one *kanban* worth of product. Shortly after the *kanban* card is printed, the cell will make the required product and get it on its way to your warehouse, thus drastically cutting your lead time and your need to carry inventory.

The cell will then send *kanban* cards to its raw material and component parts vendors to replenish what it has just used. This loop is repeated every time a customer or customers order a quantity equal to the *kanban* quantity. To maximize this system over time, you will also have to change your customers' behavior. You need to get them to stop ordering using their own MRP system (which orders in batches) and get them to just tell you every day what they have sold. You can then treat this as an order and replenish it. This will complete the *kanban* loop and tie you very tightly to your customers.

Let me emphasize that, like any key Lean principle or tool, *kanban*, or the concept of *kanban*, is just as powerful in nonmanufacturing settings. Take, for example, the time I was asked to run a *kaizen* focusing on the laundry at St. Francis Hospital in Hartford, Connecticut. This is an approximately 500-bed hospital, and I have to admit that I was quite surprised to see how big the laundry was. I mean, who even thinks about the laundry in a hospital? It had huge washing machines and an enormous machine that automatically dried and ironed sheets. The problem was that the laundry was not keeping up with the demands of its customers. The patient floors had to have the proper linens when they needed them. As a result, people started hoarding sheets and towels. They were stuffed in closets and stacked in hallways, taking up a lot of space and costing the hospital an extra $600,000 in excess linen investment. This was a perfect application for a *kanban* system. *Kanban* cards coming from the patient floors would initiate production. Carts could then be loaded with just what was needed and delivered to the proper floor. The closets could be emptied out for other purposes, and the hospital could reclaim its $600,000. As another example, at Virginia Mason Medical Center in Seattle, Washington, I saw a hyperbaric treatment department where the whole patient flow was run by *kanban*. It was very simple and very efficient, and the patients loved it.

Sustaining Your Lean Gains

Congratulations. If you have made headway on making these changes and enlisting people in the Lean work, you are on your way. Now comes more work: learning how to lead this Lean transformation so that Lean becomes the way work is done in your company—that is, your culture. Let's explore what Lean leadership means, and how you will need to change in order to build on your Lean achievements.

What Lean Leaders Do

Implementing a Lean strategy takes time. It is a journey, not a sprint. As a result, without strong, committed leadership over a long period of time, most Lean transformations will fail. Introducing Lean is one thing, but keeping it going is where the leadership work is really required. CEOs are rarely interested in such radical change in the first place (they are busy), but the real challenge comes from their need to shift from managing to leading in order to have any chance of success. As a Lean leader, you will have to lead from the front in a hands-on way. Constantly insist on the Lean fundamentals (takt time, one-piece flow, standard work, and pull). Be willing to take a lot of "leaps of faith" to achieve extraordinary results. Always challenge the company and industry lore that holds most companies back. When things go wrong, the CEO has to be the one that keeps the team going forward and the naysayers at bay.

All right, you are off and running. You have announced your new Lean strategy, lined up the Lean expertise you will need, done some training, and started your *kaizen* activity. You may have lined up a full *kaizen* schedule for the first year. There is a lot of buzz and excitement within your company. So now what? You've reached the hard part. This is where you have to switch from your current role as manager to your new role as leader. For a lot of people, this is *not* easy to do. This is why there are so few Lean leaders, and, as a result, why only 5 to 7 percent of companies are successful with a Lean transformation.

In this chapter, then, we will address the issue of leadership. We will cover some of the characteristics of a good Lean leader and discuss how to respond to the problems that will inevitably pop up. I'll also suggest a couple of simple approaches that you can use to keep everyone on your team aligned as you move through your transformation. This is important because making the switch to Lean is not like any other new program you have tried (like, say, switching to a new MRP system or a new accounting system). Programs of this type have a start point and an end point. Lean does not. Instead, it is the start of a journey that, if you do it correctly, will never end. This is why leadership is so important. Without strong, committed leadership, the Lean journey won't last very long. You'll get a few impressive gains, but then you'll slip back to where you were before. Trust me, I have been observing this for many years.

Where Are All the Lean Leaders?

Here is a good example of the issue of poor leadership, from my days at Wiremold. After some real success working with Lean, Wiremold became a little famous. A full chapter was devoted to Wiremold in the seminal book *Lean Thinking*, by James P. Womack and Daniel T. Jones, and the company was featured in a full chapter in Masaaki Imai's book *Gemba Kaizen*, as well as being mentioned in many other articles and books. Many people asked to visit our factory to see what Lean looked like. Our staff members felt obligated to help others. My team set aside time to lead plant tours and participate in long Q&A sessions. It was great for morale, but it was time-consuming. After a while, we were being overwhelmed by requests. At the same time, we were becoming convinced that devoting a day out of our lives to a company whose CEO was not interested enough to attend was probably a waste of time. If the CEO was not going to lead the Lean conversion, we thought, the rest of the management team was probably just window-shopping. So, we established a simple rule that plant tours and informational sessions would be available only to companies that brought their CEO.

Overnight, the visits stopped. There were still a lot of requests, but so few had an interested and involved CEO that the visits nearly ceased, and we got back to the business of running Wiremold.

I don't think this should be all that shocking. After all, most CEOs got to where they are by following the traditional management approach. Why should they change? Probably 95 percent of them see Lean as some "manufacturing thing" that might help their company in some way, but that could certainly be delegated to the vice president of operations. On top of all that, CEOs are busy. Perhaps you could even say that they are "too busy to get better," at least right now—maybe later. So part of the problem is to get CEOs interested in Lean in the first place (beyond some twisted idea that it will help them reduce their head count). The next hurdle is to convince them to understand Lean as a strategy (an unfair competitive weapon, if you will). And, then, hardest of all, you need to convince them that they will have to change their own style and become a leader if they are to have any success with Lean over the long haul.

Lean Leadership

In any business, the only element that is capable of true transformation is people. Machines can be moved, equipment can be reconfigured, and buildings can be sold or built, but none of these are true transformations. Only people can change in character and appreciate in value. As CEO, you need to plan for the transformation of everyone in the company—not just you and your management team. For Lean to work at the strategic level, everyone needs to think and act in a new way. This new way involves teamwork and thinking in terms of what is good for the company and the customers instead of protecting one's turf.

People, as I have noted, do not like change. And because people are pretty smart, resistance can be inventive and will come from every part of the company, from senior management to the shop floor. The strongest pressure against change, in my experience, usually comes from middle management and finance. Middle managers are simply threatened by changes in expectations, and finance usually tries desperately to defend standard cost and absorption accounting systems, even against lots of evidence showing that these systems give the wrong answers.

The only way to navigate these pressures is through strong leadership. The CEO must lead by example and consistently guide everyone back to the Lean fundamentals. The CEO must break up fiefdoms and get everyone rowing in the same direction. It is your job to identify anyone who is intractably opposed to Lean—especially in senior management—and let that person go before he becomes an immovable force against change.

All of this is easier to do if your company is in crisis—when people have a sense of urgency about changing course in order to save the organization. If bankruptcy is not threatening, the CEO needs to find another urgent situation that will help make the Lean argument. Often, there are competitive changes in your market sector or disruptive technologies that can help make a case for the urgency of transformation. There also might be glaring opportunities for improvement that could be pointed out. This is one of those vital tasks that cannot be delegated. The CEO must make the case, and keep making it.

When I was group executive at Danaher, for example, one of my companies, Veeder-Root Corporation, was already making more than 30 percent earnings before interest and taxes (EBIT) margin and was pretty smug about it. I had to point out all the waste that still existed (we were able to go from three factories to two) and the future issues that we would face if we didn't change. In other words, I had to create the case for urgency.

The Walk of Shame

One of the things that really helped me make the case for change with my Veeder-Root management team was the "walk of shame." It was one of the most powerful tools I had ever seen to get people to see the waste in their value-adding activities. My first exposure to this was at Veeder-Root's largest plant, in Elizabethtown, North Carolina. Early in our first *kaizen* week in North Carolina, Chihiro Nakao took Veeder-Root's senior management team, from the president on down, and the *kaizen* team leaders for that week on "the walk of shame." This consisted of simply walking around the plant and stopping at numerous places where Nakao, with his "Lean eyes," could point out the waste (and there was lots of it). It was especially devastating for them when we went into the internal warehouses (raw material, work in progress [WIP], and finished goods) and looked at the dates on every pallet or box of material. Some of them were two to four years old. The senior management got religion fast.

More recently, at one of my portfolio companies, Shuichi Kurosaka, who just this year became president of Shingijutsu, conducted a "walk of shame" after one of the 4 p.m. leaders' meetings. This was a big plant, so we had six teams with about 70 people on this walk. We had barely gotten started when Kurosaka-san pulled up the whole group in front of a big pile of WIP inventory. He then asked the plant manager, Bob Pugh, to give him $20. "What?" said Bob. "Just give me $20," said Kurosaka. So Bob gave him $20, and Kurosaka stuck it on the big pile of inventory. He then turned to Bob and said, "Look, you are wasting the company's money with all of this inventory, so you might as well waste some of your own as well." He then turned to the rest of the group and said, "Let's go." Poor Bob was left standing there with his mouth open, knowing that he couldn't go back and retrieve his $20. He just moved on with the rest of the group, but he got the message loud and clear and is still fond of telling this story.

I have used the "walk of shame" many times myself over the years, and it is always very effective. Often I will stand at the entrance to an internal warehouse with my index finger to my lips, telling the group as they enter, "Shh, you don't want to wake up all the 'sleeping money' that you put here." They laugh, but at the same time they are embarrassed, and they get the point. They really get it when they submit their next capital appropriation request and I tell them not to come looking for money from me when they can just go home and wake up some of their own "sleeping money."

Using the "walk of shame" or other methods to help you "see" the opportunity in your company is one thing, but it is not enough. The CEO must commit to telling this story, in person, repeatedly while spending time on the shop floor, on *kaizen* teams, in Friday report-out meetings, and while convincing the members of his senior team to join *kaizen* efforts. Everyone in the organization should know that the CEO expects them to be on *kaizen* teams regularly, learning new aspects of Lean and teamwork, until this becomes the natural method for solving problems and making improvements. When this happens, you will have a *kaizen* culture that will be hard for your competitors to beat.

Policy Deployment: *Hoshin Kanri* Planning

The most important tool for you to use in getting everyone on board and all your resources aligned behind your Lean turnaround is called policy deployment, or *hoshin kanri* planning. It is something that I recommend you implement early in your Lean journey. There has been a lot written about this approach, so I don't plan to cover it in detail here. Instead, I will give you a brief overview.

Let me begin by explaining that adopting and implementing policy deployment is a critical element in the work of a Lean leader. It is the tool that allows you to take your long-term strategic plan and deploy it in your organization. It defines the clear "breakthrough" projects that you will focus on in the current year and then aligns your leadership team and individual contributors around these projects. It also creates the accountability for making sure that these projects are given the proper resources and will get done on time.

Like a lot of other aspects of Lean, policy deployment is a visual system. It focuses on the "must-do-can't-fail" projects that you have to get done this year. It helps to prevent you from making the common mistake of trying to do ten number-one projects this year when you can do only four effectively with the resources that you have available. You will see this visually, and you will be forced to "deselect" or postpone those projects that can't be given sufficient resources.

One of the most important aspects of policy deployment is that it aligns your leadership team around a well-defined set of objectives. It helps the team stay focused on your priorities, and it creates the linkage between these initiatives and how they fit your strategy and key metrics. You will find, for example, that many of the *kaizen* projects you select will tie back to the key *hoshin* projects and your overall strategy. This way, everything is linked up, and all your resources are aligned.

To give you a sense of what this looks like visually, I have included two examples that I borrowed from Ed Miller, president and CEO of Strategy Development Services, LLC. Ed is a former colleague of mine and a true expert at policy deployment. The first chart (see Figure 7.1) shows both the top-level (company-level) development matrix (level 1) and the department- or business team–level matrix (level 2). This is a broad overview, but it shows how the company's goals (strategic objectives) are supported by common strategies (i.e., this year's strategic projects), which are then broken down further into more specific projects (i.e., *hoshin*) and then which department or business team is responsible. The level 2 matrix starts with this year's strategic projects and then moves to *hoshin* projects and subprojects, along with individual names indicating how this will be staffed.

To give you an idea of what a company-level (level 1) policy deployment matrix looks like, I have provided the second chart (see Figure 7.2). This will probably help you to understand this tool a little better, as it shows specific goals, strategies, and *hoshin* that are a little easier to relate to. The key thing to remember here is that policy deployment is a powerful leadership tool that will help you align your entire company around your Lean turnaround. I strongly recommend that you use it.

Daily Management

Lean leaders understand the critical need to establish a very strong and disciplined daily management approach at the point of value adding. If you are a manufacturing company, this will be on the shop floor. If you are a service or distribution company, this will be at the office or warehouse.

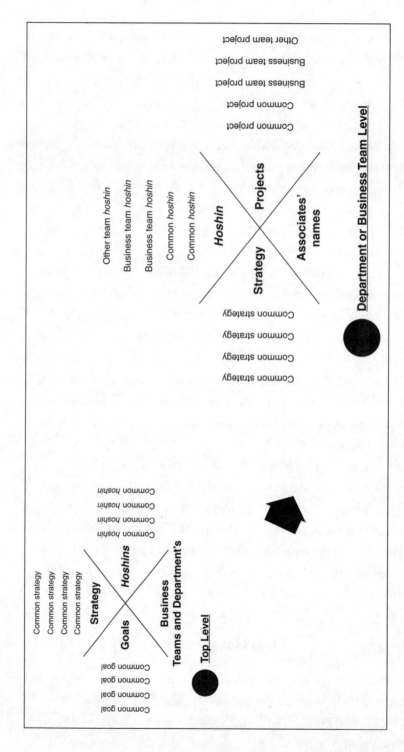

Figure 7.1 Policy Deployment "X" Matrices. (Copyright by Strategy Development Services, LLC and used with permission.)

State - Policy Deployment Matrix - Top Level (PDI)

Legend:
- ● Strong or direct impact
- ◆ Weak or no impact

Strategies (3 years)

- Tack on STRATEGIC ACQUISITIONS adding services, capabilities valued and market access in targeted markets.
- Establish new MARKET POSITIONS in targeted adjacent markets and selected geographical regions leveraging and investing in our unique competencies offering complete solutions and services providing a one-stop shop.
- Compete on SPEED to market with short-industry leading lead times, material velocity to customers with products that are the simplest and quickest to install and use.
- Develop steam of new product platforms and derivatives for application-specific use and customer benefit utilizing QFD getting the VOC and achieving a 70% shorter day time.
- Establish LEAN BUSINESS SYSTEM enterprisewide, based on continuous improvement, establishing standard work in all processes and committed to the total elimination of vesta.

Key Metrics & Goals (3–5 years)

- Operational Excellence: Defect reduction: 60% per year, Labor productivity: > 20% imp. per year, Mat Velocity (Inv): > 20 turns
- Financial Performance: EBITDA = 15%, 20% imp. per year Working capital turns:<10, 10% imp. per year, PROFIT SHARING: 20% of base pay
- Balanced Revenue Growth: Sales: > 15% per year
- Innovation: 35% current-year sales from new products introduced over last 4 years
- Great place to Work: People EAS: 10% imp. per year, Safety = 0 recordables, 100% implementation
- Customer Satisfaction: OTD: 98% first shipment Response Time: 100% all goals, 10% imp. per year

Center labels

- Hoshin (Key initiatives)
- Key Strategies (Breakthroughs)
- Key Metrics Goals (3 Years & Current Year)
- Team Support

Corporate Hoshins / Hoshins (now focus)

- Install Real-time full system from customer order through operations MOS/TTI: *Kanban* system/in place, Inventory turns double (12 mo.) LDR: Frank M
- Develop new rigid packaging platform MOS/TTI: 5 min. change over, 20% imp. in speed, payback in 12 mo. in 30% smaller footprint LDR: Hillary R
- Develop South American benchmark MOS: In-region footprint, sales coverage and aligned product offering, achieve 5 MM Sales by 2013 LDR: Larry N
- ADD Plastic Processing capabilities and valid market position MOS:ID 5 companies to pursue - build acquisition tunnel, close 1 in 18 mo. LDR: Jack W

Teams / Departments

- Executive team
- Admin. (Finance, IT, HR)
- Rigid Packaging VST
- Plastic Assemblies VST
- Aftermarket VST
- Global R&D / Engineering team
- Supply Chain Management Team
- Marketing Team
- Sales Team
- Operations Support Team

Legend:
- ⊙ - Leader
- ● - High Impact / Strong Support
- ● - Some Impact / Moderate Support
- ◆ - Weak or No Impact

Figure 7.2 Policy Deployment Matrix (PD1). (Copyright by Strategy Development Services, LLC and used with permission.)

It needs to include visual controls at the point of value adding that track the critical metrics that tie back to the company's strategy and financial goals. Your focus has to be on process improvement to eliminate waste. And so you should measure those things that will tell you whether you are eliminating waste from your value-adding activities: things like productivity (pieces per person-hour), setup reduction (trend in minutes), reduction in defects (as a percentage), and shortening your lead time to your customers. Or, if you are a hospital, you might track the percentages of discharges that occurred on time, reduction in waiting time in the Emergency Room, turnaround time for an MRI or from the blood lab, and overall patient safety and satisfaction.

These data should be posted at least hourly by the people who do the value-adding or their supervisors. Once you are collecting the right information, there should be a daily walk-around meeting in each cell or work area to review the data, talk about countermeasures, and initiate action immediately if necessary. The CEO should participate in these daily walk-around meetings as much as possible and should always make a point of reviewing the visual data and asking questions when he is in the *gemba*. A graphic view of how this should affect your organization in terms of time spent is shown in Figure 7.3.

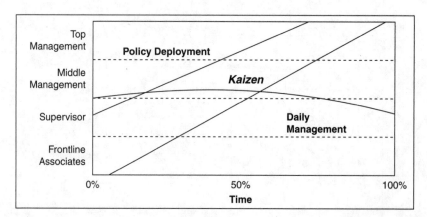

Figure 7.3 Why Daily Management?

Lean Leadership and Leaps of Faith

Being a Lean leader is a lot like being a player coach. You are on the team, creating the strategy and giving guidance, but your biggest contribution is to lead by the example that you set through your own play on the field (or, in our case, in the *gemba*). The Lean leader needs to put the primary focus on where you are going, not where you have been. This means concentrating on all your processes to remove the waste. Remember, the winners will be those who focus on their processes, not their results. Be vigilant everywhere: cut the lead time, improve the quality, increase the flexibility, lower the cost, and strengthen the link to the customer in every process you have (whether in the office or the factory).

This means that you have to be the company Lean zealot. The more your people recognize your complete commitment, the more they will respond and improve. Part of this role will require you to always be challenging the current state. "We have 10 people on this line; why can't we do it with 3?" "This setup takes 14 hours, but we need to get it under 10 minutes." "Why does it take five days to turn a quote around? We have to be able to respond in one day or less." "Why are we still making order entry errors? When will they be eliminated?" Push for these changes. And at the same time, congratulate your associates on their achievements while helping them recognize the next challenge. Celebrate each new gain, but keep moving forward.

One of the bigger challenges for most CEOs is that Lean requires a lot of leaps of faith, something that many leaders find uncomfortable. When we first started working with Shingijutsu at Danaher Corporation, George Koenigsaecker and I made a decision (sort of a pact) that whatever our Japanese consultants told us to do, we would "just do it." This was a little scary for both of us because they were constantly asking us to do things that we really questioned. On the other hand, we wanted to learn, and we had to get better or there would be no Jake Brake. Just about everything we did was in the "leap of faith" category because the "but what if it doesn't work?" question was always in the background. As it turned out, even when we ran into problems (and this happened a lot), we always came out better in the end. For us, the "just do it" approach was the right one. It will be the right one for you as well.

Taking leaps of faith will be harder for some CEOs than for others. We all have different personality types and different management styles. The insecure CEO and the command-and-control CEO will find this especially difficult. They want to control all the outcomes beforehand (or at least have someone to blame). With Lean leaps of faith, however, you are always taking a risk (jumping into the unknown) in order to make a dramatic improvement in some process. I can certainly understand how these CEOs are thinking. On the other hand, I know that this type of timidity can be overcome if you try. Let's say that the Lean leader wants to reduce defects by 50 percent per year, but the traditional manager doesn't want to set any goal that he can't beat, so he sets a target of reducing defects by 5 percent. At the end of the year, the traditional manager achieves a 7.5 percent reduction in defects (150 percent of plan) and the Lean leader misses his target by 20 percent, so he gets only a 40 percent reduction in defects. Who really won here? It's pretty easy to see. Over time, the Lean leader will crush the traditional manager, even if he keeps falling a little short of his goal.

So, let your guard down and take the leap of faith when it presents itself. If you don't quite succeed, regroup, figure out what went wrong, and leap again. At all costs, make sure that you never blame anyone if the leap of faith doesn't quite work out. A blame environment (i.e., "Who did that?") is totally incompatible with Lean. As CEO, you are the one who has to set the tone here.

Fight Industry Lore

In addition to making leaps of faith, the Lean leader has to be the one to break the paradigms that tend to exist in any business. These may be company-specific, but they might be industry lore as well. Industry lore gets passed on from company to company as individuals change jobs, and it gets entrenched and accepted over time. If your company is looking for a new vice president of operations or a new vice president of sales, for example, chances are very high that one of the key qualifications you will be looking for is "industry experience." This is nice, but it just perpetuates the lore of how things are done.

Let me share an example of this. Years ago, I was on the board of a jewelry manufacturer that had asked me for some help. I visited the company and asked, "How long does it take to make a ring?" The people at the company said that it takes eight weeks, which is the standard in the industry (which, by the way, I later confirmed). As I will tell you in more detail later, in a short period of time, with no real capital investment, I was able to change this lead time to two days. This was no stroke of genius on my part. I just wasn't infected with the industry lore that said that it had to take eight weeks.

I have a similar situation now with one of my portfolio companies where I am chairman. It is in the printing business, and it has a lot of lore (both company and industry) that is holding it back. It is a really great group of people, so I know we will be very successful here eventually. Getting these people to look outside the lore and see the possibilities that I see, however, is taking some time. It's very easy for them to listen to me, but then ignore what I'm telling them. They tell themselves, "Well, Art doesn't come from this industry, so he just doesn't know." I keep reminding them that they are "only putting ink on paper," so let's keep it simple. (This, of course, drives them nuts because they want to see themselves as much more sophisticated than that.) At the same time, we are making progress in breaking down the barriers (inventory turns have more than doubled, lead times have come down, working capital turns have increased from 6 times to more than 100 times, and margins are up more than 30 percent). My point here is that changing company lore may take you some time, but as CEO, you have to stick with it and keep pushing. It is just another key aspect of Lean leadership.

Three Steps Forward—Two Steps Back

Some of the biggest challenges you will face as a Lean leader will come when things go wrong. I can guarantee you that as soon as there is a problem, you will hear from all the naysayers on your staff and in the rest of the company: "I told you this wouldn't work here." Unless you already have a few strong Lean converts or some Lean backing from your board of directors, you will be standing there all alone. What should you do? If you blink now, you lose. Wiremold had actually tried Lean before I arrived. It had run into problems and fled back to its old batch ways (in fact, it built even bigger batches). But in fairness, this is more the norm than the exception. Your leadership will be tested every time you run into problems, and you will run into problems. In fact, I'd like to point out some of the more common ones so that you will be prepared.

In most of the Lean conversions that I have been involved with, progress could be described as three steps forward and two steps back. This happens because the changes being made are so different from the prior way of working and because there is a lot of discipline required in Lean that was not previously required. If you can achieve three steps forward and only one step back, you will outperform almost everyone. Be aware that backward steps are very common. Your leadership will be required to minimize them and allow your team to keep making progress.

For instance, traditional companies generally do a bad job of maintaining equipment (they run it until it breaks). When you put ill-kept machines into a one-piece-flow cell, it suddenly becomes glaringly obvious that these machines cannot hold a tolerance or run reliably. This shuts down production. Or suppose you are a bank and you develop a one-piece-flow process to reduce the time it takes to turn a loan application around, but your computer system crashes as a result of the changes that were made and customers are affected. This will give all the skeptics in your organization plenty of ammunition to argue, "Lean won't work here." As the leader, you have to intercede here. Get the machines fixed, establish a total productive maintenance (TPM) program, and keep going forward.

Or, let's say you plan to move Product A into a cellular configuration, and you have some stock built to cover the week during which the machines will be moving. But this is the week when customers bury you in orders for Product A (very tricky these customers). Scrambling ensues, and probably a few stock-outs. Likewise, overestimating what new one-piece-flow cells can produce when going into a peak season without building enough safety stock is also likely to result in stock-outs. These are short-term customer service problems, but I can almost guarantee that you will have them. Once again, your leadership is needed to keep your team focused on where you are going. How will you solve these problems without reverting to a big inventory buildup (or going back to the old way of processing loan applications)? This is the stuff that happens as you scramble to get better. It is not something that should make you stop your move to Lean. In fact, I always looked at these types of issues as the reason I needed to go faster in the Lean conversion so that I could get to the state where I could make them go away.

Another issue you will have has no simple fix: getting everyone to adhere to standard work. There will always be a few associates—at every level of an organization—who are incredibly reluctant to follow standard work. Don't expect to solve this overnight, either. This one will test not only your leadership, but also your perseverance. You have to constantly stay on top of this.

Another people hazard is taking away chairs from the shop floor. For the people in the new one-piece-flow cells who have now been trained to run multiple machines and move between operations, a chair makes no sense. Even the more stationary operators, however, will need to make the switch to standing. This is better for the body and better for work flow (not to mention being about 20 percent more efficient), but be prepared for pushback, and take the time to prepare operators for the new working style. They will need to hear it from you. The real issue here involves asking people to change their physical approach to the job. In office environments, sitting may still be necessary, but try to make sure that paperwork can flow (be handed) from one person to the next.

Union environments with lots of job classifications are often more difficult for *kaizen* implementation. Union leaders may resist having salaried employees working alongside union members during *kaizen* weeks. You will have to work out accommodations with the union. At Wiremold, we finally achieved an agreement that *kaizen* work was intended to improve processes for everyone, save the company, and increase profit sharing; therefore, *kaizen* teams enjoyed special dispensation from union rules.

Smooth operation of a pull system is difficult. *Kanban* cards can get lost, and leaders cannot see the demand, causing stock-outs. It will take time to train everyone to treat a *kanban* card like it's a $50 bill, so that it does not get lost, and so that it enables the pull system to reflect customer demand reliably. You will probably have some customer service problems in the early stages of your *kanban* system implementation. The naysayers will be up in arms. Just keep in mind that the whole reason you are doing this is to improve customer service. Fix the problems and lead your team forward.

Overcoming these problems is critical to your success. There are no pat solutions, but the CEO's reaction is key. Some people in your organization will try to use each bump in the road as an excuse or an illustration of why Lean does not work. It is your job to remind everyone that all of this—the stock-outs, customer service issues, and rebellions on the shop floor when you take away the chairs—are all just problems to be worked out. Do not allow backsliding or excuses.

Lean Leaders' Standard Work

Lean leaders must follow their own standard work to ensure that they can turn around their company or organization successfully using the Lean approach. The best presentation I have ever seen on the subject of a leader's standard work occurred recently at a CEO *kaizen* event at one of my portfolio companies. Don Doles, a former colleague of mine at Danaher Corporation (he was part of the first "presidents' *kaizen*" events, so he goes way back), and I have been working together facilitating these events for the past year and a half. At the last one, he gave a presentation on leaders' standard work to the company's senior management team. I can't cover it all here, but a brief summary will give you the basics.

Lean Leaders' Standard Work

- Set the direction and build organizational capability to solve problems at the root cause.
- Support the important processes through daily *gemba* walks and frequent reviews of the key performance indicators (KPI).
- Identify breakthrough opportunities and set stretch goals to achieve them.
- Show respect and support for all your associates.

Don even created a very simple graphic, which I have included as Figure 7.4.

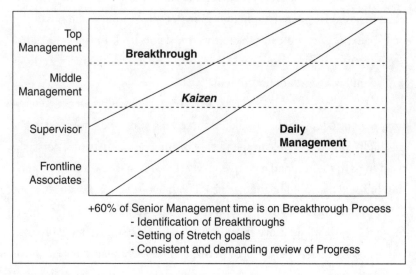

Figure 7.4 Leader's Standard Work

Creating Your Future Leaders

Planning for your succession and that of the members of your senior team is a key role for the leader of any business. This is true under a Lean strategy as well. The only new wrinkle that Lean adds to this equation is that in order to move up in a Lean organization, it should be mandatory that the person have had hands-on Lean experience. If your role as CEO is to be the company's Lean zealot, then in order to continue the Lean progress into the future, you have to be grooming the future zealots. If I put in an individual to run one of my divisions, I never have to worry about whether he will be driving Lean forward every day. I want to be sure that he has the hands-on Lean experience on the shop floor (or, in service companies, at the point of value creation) as a minimum. I want to know that he is fully capable of running a *kaizen* event himself, and that he knows how to pick and run other *kaizen* events. I need to be confident that he understands Lean as the strategy and, most important, that he is a team player who will respect everyone in the organization. I may have some questions or reservations about his overall experience or business acumen, but I can't have any question about whether he will be driving Lean every day.

The good news here is that, for the most part, once a person has been in a real Lean environment for any length of time and has had the proper exposures, he can't make the transition back into a traditional organization. It just won't make sense to him any longer. Everything will seem backward and inefficient.

At Wiremold, to address this issue of bringing along the next generation, we attacked it from a number of directions. First of all, we tried to get our high-potential people to spend a lot of time on *kaizen* teams. Next, we tried to have them spend a couple of years working in the *kaizen* promotion office. This could be followed by a couple of years as a value-stream leader where they had full responsibility for one of our product lines. From there, we might move them into the sales force for a couple of years to get commercial experience, or perhaps make them plant managers. We also took regional sales managers who expressed an interest in running one of our businesses someday (and whom we thought could do it) and made them plant managers at some of our smaller subsidiaries so that they could get the hands-on Lean experience that we required. I even had my vice president of engineering run one of our factories for two years (where he reported to the vice president of operations—one of his peers) while keeping his engineering role because he had expressed a strong interest in running a business, but needed the hands-on Lean knowledge.

In addition to these steps, you as CEO have to ensure that your senior team really works as a team. When the team members come together, they should be making decisions about the company, not just about their particular function. When someone asks the team members a question, they should be able to give an answer that reflects what the company is doing, not just what their function thinks. This means that any management team member can comment on any subject (in any functional area) and be listened to and respected. This may take you a little time to achieve, but part of your future succession planning should be to have a cohesive management team in place that would continue on the same Lean path without any question if you were to get hit by the proverbial bus.

The Value-Adding CEO

Part of your conversion from manager to Lean leader requires that you understand the concept of value-added and non-value-added in your company. While the traditional CEO sits in his office looking at the numbers, the Lean CEO should be on the shop floor working to understand and eliminate the non-value-adding activities. As an example here, I have often said that if you let me spend a week on the shop floor of any company (or where value is added in a nonmanufacturing company)—even one I am unfamiliar with—at the end of that week, I will most likely know more about the issues and opportunities facing that company than its CEO does. This is not because I am some sort of wizard. I am not. In fact, any person with a deep understanding of Lean would be able to do the same thing. Why this is true is the lesson to be learned here.

The key is that my whole week at the point of value creation will be focused on separating value-adding activities from non-value-adding activities. Doing this makes it easy to see the problems in current operations—the poor productivity, bad quality, long lead times, piles of inventory, and so on—and options for eliminating those issues. In the office, there may be big piles of paper in in- and out-boxes, poor housekeeping, and no visual controls. As improvements are implemented, the Lean CEO can also see how the company can better serve customers, improve quality, lower costs, and begin to utilize the freed-up space and cash. Simply being immersed in the details and really understanding how value is added will give the CEO all the insight required.

The lesson here is that success in a Lean conversion requires new habits on the part of the CEO. You have to see yourself as being value-adding and not just part of the overhead waste. Put your attention on understanding and removing the non-value-adding activities. This means that you have to get out of your office and go observe them. You don't want to be in a position where someone like me could spend a week immersed in your value-adding activities and know more about your strategic opportunities than you do. The good news is that CEOs who make the hard choices and change old habits, win.

Tracking Progress

Without measurement, it is impossible for you to assess your Lean efforts. Therefore, it is critical that, in addition to your daily management system, you create simple higher-level data-tracking sheets, with results being reported to you at least monthly. Keep in mind that people respond to what is measured, and that these reports should allow you to focus on the more important Lean metrics in a simple and consistent way.

To help you visualize this, I have reproduced the monthly tracking sheets that we use in one of my high-volume consumer products portfolio companies. This organization has been doing an excellent job in its

Lean conversion, and Table 7.1 shows the two-page monthly tracking report used at the plant level. This privately held company has 12 plants in Europe alone, so we want to be able to compare progress across plants. There are some sales and expense data shown here, but you will see that the main focus is on key Lean measurements: inventory turns, productivity, customer service, scrap reduction (quality), setup reduction, standard work, and pull systems. All of this rolls up from the daily management data at the cell level. The company also tracks space savings, stock-keeping unit (SKU) reduction, and the number of *kaizen* events conducted. Inventory turns and customer service are the most important measures. When these items are both trending upward, things are moving in the right direction. When measures change direction for the worse, the tracking document helps leaders respond quickly and accurately focus future improvement work.

The monthly review of these plant reports should not be lengthy or time-consuming. It is a quick assessment and an opportunity to plan improvements. Then, once a year, all plant managers and senior functional business heads gather to discuss the annual results on these measures and set goals for the next year. This creates an atmosphere of teamwork, while at the same time providing a little friendly competition to get better. No one wants to stand up at such a meeting and show that his plant has had the worst results.

The third sheet, Table 7.2, shows the monthly measurement sheet for the same company at the corporate level. This sheet includes more financial data, but we also focus on working capital turns and productivity. Having a 13-month data array in each case offers a quick snapshot of Lean progress, as well as an illustration of seasonal fluctuations resulting from the company's external markets. These tools offer at-a-glance progress checks, as well as a look ahead at where the trendlines are leading, and should help you manage your business more proactively. In fact, I believe that you can run your entire business using just these three sheets. For service companies, the information you track may be slightly different, but the concept is the same. Track those processes that will have the most impact on your future strategic and financial success.

Table 7.1 Monthly Tracking Report: Plant Level

Unit #: 4942 Date: July 9, 2010	List currency USD													Exchange Rate 1,32979	
Person responsible for Mfg or Inventory:	Jul-09	Aug-09	Sep-09	Oct-09	Nov-09	Dec-09	Jan-10	Feb-10	Mar-10	Apr-10	May-10	Jun-10	Jul-10	YTD	YE Target
Sales															
Sales (produced at facility) in 000s	4,015	3,335	5,976	4,653	6,041	8,757	6,060	3,378	3,791	2,951	2,943	2,008	2,011	23,141	55,186
Operating Plant Expenses															
In 000s	1,307	1,145	1,323	1,234	814	945	750	995	803	774	652	791	828	5,593	13,797
As % of sales	33%	34%	22%	27%	13%	11%	12%	29%	21%	26%	22%	21%	41%	24%	25%
Variance from prior year %	-9.5%	-13.8%	-2.7%	-17.9%	-54.1%	-33.2%	-89.0%	-32.1%	-51.3%	-52.9%	-89.4%	-49.9%	-18.7%	-1.5%	-2.0%
Inventory—12-month rolling average															
Raw material	307	316	323	323	326	316	316	316	303	293	283	269	254	254	199
WIP & semifinished	11	9	8	8	8	8	8	9	8	8	9	9	7	7	7
Finished goods (all F/Gs that you are responsible for)	2,980	2,810	2,634	2,398	2,156	2,084	1,984	1,874	1,868	1,842	1,811	1,717	1,747	1,747	1,795
Total inventory—raw, WIP, finished (PUDC & MDC)	3,298	3,136	2,965	2,729	2,489	2,408	2,309	2,199	2,180	2,142	2,104	1,995	2,008	2,008	2,001
Total inventory—raw, WIP, finished (PUDC & MDC), month end	2,081	1,765	1,547	3,215	4,441	2,906	1,874	1,419	1,313	1,254	1,008	1,113	2,273	2,273	2,015
Inventory Turns															
PUDC & MDC of own production only (raw, WIP & FG)															
Turns (last 12-month cost of goods sold divided by 12-month average Inv.)	14.5	15.0	15.3	16.0	16.3	15.3	15.5	16.0	15.7	15.8	15.8	16.7	16.2	16.2	18.1
Month-end Inventory turns	23.0	26.6	29.3	13.6	9.1	12.7	17.9	24.9	26.1	27.0	32.9	30.0	14.3	14.3	17.3
Number of Raw Material SKUs															
Number of raw material SKUs (all components, boxes, & labels)	250	250	250	250	250	250	250	250	250	250	250	250	250	250	250
Pull Systems															
The # of machines or cells that build to a pull signal	4	5	5	5	5	5	5	5	5	5	5	5	5	5	5
% of volume that is mfg. to a pull system	100%	100%	100%	100%	100%	100%	100%	100%	100%	100%	100%	100%	100%	100%	100%
Plant Head Count (Site Only)															
Salaried	12	12	11	11	11	11	11	11	10	10	10	10	10	10	10
Hourly	87	87	87	87	87	87	85	83	76	75	74	75	75	75	77
Temporary	0	0	0	5	5	4	0	0	0	0	0	0	0	0	4
Total plant head count	99	99	99	103	103	102	96	94	86	85	84	85	85	85	91
Subcontracted FTE heads for the month	1	1	1	2	3	3	3	2	2	2	2	1	1	1	0
Total overtime hours	-882	529	879	1,108	1,113	530	571	-2,314	-1,042	-900	-500	-300	-228	-228	0
Productivity															
Sales/employee last 12 months sales/end of month FTE	645	636	614	582	573	543	577	590	644	648	653	654	653	653	606

Table 7.1 (Continued)

Unit #: 4942 Date: July 9, 2010	List currency USD														Exchange Rate 1.32979	
Person responsible for Mfg. or Inventory:	Jul-09	Aug-09	Sep-09	Oct-09	Nov-09	Dec-09	Jan-10	Feb-10	Mar-10	Apr-10	May-10	Jun-10	Jul-10	YTD	YE Target
Plant and DC *Kaizen* Activity															
# of *kaizen*	11	7	9	5	4	3	9	5	3	6	3	5	4	35	60
% of people in at least two *kaizen* (cumulative all *kaizen*)	98%	98%	98%	98%	98%	98%	98%	98%	98%	98%	98%	98%	98%	98%	100%
# of *kaizen* promotion office people	2.5	2.5	2.5	2.0	2.0	2.0	2.0	2.0	2.0	2.0	2.0	2.0	2.0	2.0	2
Space															
Total square meters within the plant (no outside warehouse space)	24,300	24,300	24,300	24,300	24,300	24,300	24,300	24,300	24,300	24,300	24,300	24,300	24,300	24,300	24,300
Total square meters of any outside space rented (include warehouse)	0	0	0	0	0	0	0	0	0	0	0	0	0	0	0
Space Savings															
Square meters space freed up (cum. each month) from Sept. 2002	10,800	10,800	10,800	10,800	10,800	10,800	10,800	10,800	10,800	10,800	10,800	10,800	10,800	10,800	12,500
Net square meters of free space (space that can be used)	10,800	10,800	10,800	10,800	10,800	10,800	10,800	10,800	10,800	10,800	10,800	10,800	10,800	10,800	12,500
Scrap Reduction															
Scrap %	0.9%	1.1%	0.7%	0.7%	0.8%	0.7%	0.8%	0.9%	0.9%	0.9%	1.0%	0.9%	0.7%	0.9%	0.8%
Setup Reduction															
# of machines total	11	11	11	11	11	11	11	11	11	11	11	11	11	11	11
. # of machines with reduced or no changeover time (cum. #)	10	10	10	10	10	10	10	10	10	10	10	10	10	10	10
. # of machines that are achieving + or - 10% of reduced setup times	8	8	8	8	8	8	8	8	8	8	8	8	8	8	10
Cells, Standard Work, & Visuals															
# of cells created each month (Cum #)	5	5	5	5	5	5	5	5	5	5	5	5	5	5	5
. # of cells or machines with posted std. work and working to it	4	4	4	4	4	4	3	4	4	4	4	4	4	4	5
. # of machines that are tracking reliability	5	5	5	5	5	5	5	5	5	5	5	5	5	5	5
. # of cells or machines that are achieving 100% of the reliability target	0	0	1	0	1	1	0	0	0	0	1	0	1	0	5
. # of cells or machines that are recording and posting scrap daily visually at cell	5	5	5	5	5	5	5	5	5	5	5	5	5	5	5
Customer Service (based on locally produced product only)															
Service level in %	98%	99%	95%	91%	96%	93%	92%	96%	96%	96%	97%	92%	97%	95%	97%

Table 7.2 Monthly Tracking Report: Corporate Level

Unit no 9000 · Period 7 · Currency USD

USD 000s	Full Yr. Actual 2009	YTD Jul 2010	Jul 2009	Aug 2009	Sep 2009	Oct 2009	Nov 2009	Dec 2009	Jan 2010	Feb 2010	Mar 2010	Apr 2010	May 2010	Jun 2010	Jul 2010	Full Yr. Budget 2010
									Month Only							
SALES (External)	902,879	481,095	84,870	77,310	83,925	81,031	84,625	97,492	64,705	55,295	70,068	60,087	63,771	85,841	81,328	903,682
Variance from prior year		0.5%	−15.3%	−17.1%	−18.2%	−17.4%	−9.6%	−11.8%	−1.3%	−4.7%	4.7%	−0.6%	3.7%	4.8%	−4.2%	
Variance from budget		0.1%							−0.1%	−3.7%	6.4%	−0.6%	0.3%	1.7%	−3.6%	
AGP %	28.6%	29.6%	28.0%	27.0%	30.6%	31.8%	31.4%	29.4%	31.8%	28.0%	33.8%	30.0%	30.2%	27.4%	26.8%	29.1%
Deviation from prior year		2.3 pts	8.8 pts	9.2 pts	11.6 pts	12.6 pts	10.3 pts	10.4 pts	4.2 pts	2.6 pts	6.9 pts	3.4 pts	2.0 pts	−0.5 pts	−1.1 pts	
Deviation from budget		0.0 pts							0.8 pts	−1.2 pts	2.9 pts	−0.5 pts	−0.3 pts	−0.9 pts	−1.1 pts	
OPERATING EXPENSES	214,494	118,714	17,675	18,007	17,471	19,799	19,866	20,364	15,309	14,210	17,059	17,402	17,233	18,785	18,716	215,376
Deviation from prior year—B(W)		273	(818)	(2,042)	(702)	(3,916)	(4,793)	(3,817)	374	1,396	345	349	(373)	(777)	(1,041)	
Variance from budget—B(W)		2.0%							0.8%	4.0%	−0.2%	4.4%	3.4%	−0.4%	2.1%	
EBITDA	74,782	41,309	8,600	5,344	11,951	8,460	9,207	11,459	7,626	3,182	8,799	3,348	4,548	7,726	6,080	82,057
Deviation from prior year		12,948	3,827	2,272	6,828	3,338	2,926	4,706	3,083	1,891	5,755	2,817	1,633	289	(2,520)	
Variance from budget		3.1%							14.7%	−19.8%	43.0%	10.7%	5.4%	−8.3%	−19.2%	
HEADCOUNT																
General & administrative	299				299			299			276			274		363
Manufacturing	3,851				3,889			3,851			3,119			3,848		3,867
Commercial	1,229				1,245			1,229			1,185			1,204		1,112
Total FTE number of employees	5,379	5,283	5,296	5,366	5,434	5,453	5,499	5,379	3,470	3,467	4,580	4,554	4,518	5,326	5,283	5,341
FTE of paid overtime	345	184	152	171	306	312	370	345	453	192	572	369	407	218	184	137
Total FTEs	5,724	5,467	5,448	5,536	5,739	5,755	5,869	5,724	3,923	3,659	5,152	4,923	4,925	5,545	5,467	5,478
Productivity (LTM sales Per FTE)	158	166	179	174	164	160	156	158	230	245	175	183	184	164	166	165
Working capital turns Month	6.9 ×	6.4 ×	6.8 ×	7.1 ×	6.9 ×	7.0 ×	6.8 ×	7.3 ×	13.2 ×	13.1 ×	9.8 ×	9.8 ×	9.6 ×	6.6 ×	6.4 ×	7.2 ×
12-mth average		8.0 ×	6.3 ×	6.4 ×	6.5 ×	6.6 ×	6.8 ×	6.9 ×	7.2 ×	7.4 ×	7.6 ×	7.8 ×	7.9 ×	8.0 ×	8.0 ×	
Inventory turns Month	6.9 ×	6.3 ×	7.0 ×	7.2 ×	7.1 ×	6.7 ×	6.5 ×	6.6 ×	13.2 ×	13.6 ×	9.6 ×	9.1 ×	8.9 ×	6.1 ×	6.3 ×	7.9 ×
12-mth average		7.6 ×	6.5 ×	6.5 ×	6.6 ×	6.7 ×	6.9 ×	6.9 ×	7.1 ×	7.3 ×	7.4 ×	7.5 ×	7.5 ×	7.6 ×	7.6 ×	
Accounts receivable days Month	50 days	51 days	51 days	53 days	50 days	48 days	49 days	45 days	41 days	41 days	48 days	50 days	53 days	49 days	51 days	50 days
12-mth average		48 days	51 days	51 days	51 days	51 days	51 days	50 days	50 days	50 days	49 days	49 days	48 days	48 days	48 days	
Accounts payable days Month	40 days	45 days	41 days	41 days	38 days	44 days	44 days	45 days	35 days	37 days	37 days	38 days	44 days	45 days	45 days	39 days
12-mth average		41 days	40 days	40 days	40 days	40 days	40 days	40 days	40 days	41 days	41 days	41 days	41 days	41 days	41 days	

Company R is not included for January – February 2009 & 2010.
Company A is not included for January – May 2009 & 2010.

How Lean Changes *Everything*

Of all the excess baggage that traditional companies carry—cumbersome capital appropriation request processes, end-of-month financial reviews, material resource planning (MRP) systems, and direct/indirect labor measures—the most intractable is standard-cost accounting. This system encourages much of the bad behavior you will be working hard to eliminate. It is the number one thing you do not need, and I strongly suggest that you convert to Lean accounting methods as soon as possible.

Converting to Lean changes everything. Not everything has to change right away, however. In fact, some things can't change until you have taken some initial steps (such as getting your value-adding activity into a one-piece flow). Even so, you can help yourself a lot if you understand some of the most critical things to change before you begin.

One of the primary responsibilities of Lean leadership is to identify and eliminate the obstacles to your success. One of the biggest mistakes that companies make during the transition to a Lean strategy is keeping existing systems and measurements in place and trying to just lay Lean on top of them. This is the normal approach for CEOs who view Lean as some "manufacturing thing." Unfortunately, approaching Lean this way pretty much guarantees that you will not be successful.

In this chapter, I will cover a number of the traditional systems and measurements that you must change as your transformation progresses. The first one on the list is the most important for you to get done early on. It will also be the most difficult, as I expect you will get lots of resistance to any changes. You will need all of your Lean leadership skills for this one. I'm talking about the need to change your accounting system; more specifically, to stop using a standard-cost absorption system.

At Wiremold, we helped a lot of companies get started down the Lean path. Quite a few of them would call up a year later and ask if they could send their vice president of finance and a couple of his key people to visit with us. The problem was that finance was resisting the change to Lean, and management was hoping that we could help the finance people see the light. I saw another example of this just recently. We (J. W. Childs Associates) were visiting a company we were thinking of buying. It gave us a big pitch on how it had been working on Lean for 10 years. The people used all the right words, but it didn't make sense—the balance sheet showed that inventory turns were still only about five times. The reason for this contradictory result was that the company had tried to do Lean *and* keep its standard-cost system in place. The standard-cost system, of course, was winning the battle. I don't want you to make the same mistake.

Standard-Cost Accounting

Standard-cost accounting systems are incompatible with Lean. They are antithetical to Lean practice because they encourage and reward precisely the behaviors that you want to eliminate. In fact, I think of standard-cost accounting as "the anti-Lean." For instance, in a Lean world, inventory is considered the root of all evil because it hides waste. The standard-cost absorption accounting method takes the opposite view: it rewards those who build inventory, allowing them to defer a portion of their production costs to a later period.

Dig a little deeper and you will find that absorption accounting also twists behavior by making shop-floor managers more interested in hitting their absorption goals for the month than in making what the customers want. In most shops, managers know exactly which products represent the most absorption hours and, come the end of the month, if they are running behind on absorption hours, production will switch over to those high-absorption products—usually built only to populate inventory racks—so that the monthly profit and loss (P&L) statement looks good.

Added to that, standard-cost accounting simply is not very accurate. In my experience, it is unusual to find a standard cost for any product that is within 30 percent of where it ought to be. When I give presentations on Lean, I always ask the audience how many of them believe that their standard-cost system is accurate. No hands go up. The problem is, standard-cost accounting contains too many assumptions and allocations based on those assumptions that are easily disproved by a simple reality check. How can a CEO make good decisions without accurate information?

Looking at a typical standard-cost P&L statement, as shown in Figure 8.1,[1] it is not hard to see how management ends up making poor decisions. In this example, sales increased over the prior year, from

	This Year	Last Year
Net sales	$ 100,000	$ 90,000
Cost of sales:		
Standard costs	48,000	45,000
Purch. price var.	(3,000)	10,000
Matl. usage var.	(2,000)	5,000
Labor eff var.	7,000	(8,000)
Labor rate var.	(2,000)	9,000
OH volume var.	2,000	2,000
OH spend var.	(2,000)	8,000
OH eff var.	16,000	(17,000)
Total cost of sales	64,000	54,000
Gross profit	$ 36,000	$ 36,000
Gross profit %	36.0%	40.0%

Useless management information

Figure 8.1 Standard-Cost P&L Statement. (Copyright 2008 by Orest J. Fiume. All rights reserved. Used with permission.)

$90 million to $100 million, while gross profit stayed the same and gross margin percentage declined from 40 percent to 36 percent. Beyond that, this statement does not tell us much. There are seven different categories of variance to look at, but how do you know whether the problem was in operations or whether it was a miscalculation in budgeting? What this P&L statement is really illustrating is how the finance staff and the companies' leadership make assumptions and set standards in the first place. The true problems remain hidden.

(This assumes that there were no price increases or cost inflation, for the sake of clarity in this example.)

The next illustration, Figure 8.2,[2] is a new statement that I call the Lean P&L statement. This shows the same company and the same results

	This Year	LastYear	+(−)%
Net sales	$100,000	$90,000	11.1
Cost of sales:			
Purchases	28,100	34,900	
Inventory (Inc.) Dec.: Mat1. Content	3,600	(6,000)	
Total materials	31,700	28,900	9.7
Processing costs:			
Factory wages	11,400	11,500	(0.9)
Factory salaries	2,100	2,000	5.0
Factory benefits	7,000	5,000	40.0
Services & sup.	2,400	2,500	(8.0)
Equipment depr.	2,000	1,900	5.3
Scrap	2,600	4,000	(35)
Total processing costs	27,500	26,900	2.2
Occupancy costs:			
Building depr.	200	200	0.0
Building services	2,200	2,000	10.0
Total occupancy costs:	2,400	2,200	9.1
Total mfg. costs	61,600	58,000	6.2
Manufacturing gross profit	38,400	32,000	20.0
Inv. Incr. (Dec.): labor, OH Content	(2,400)	4,000	
GAAP gross profit	36,000	36,000	0.0
	36.0%	40.0%	

Figure 8.2 Lean (Plain English) P&L Statement. (Copyright 2008 by
Orest J. Fiume. All rights reserved. Used with permission.)

as the previous statement. Now, however, you can see some unvarnished reality at a glance. Materials as a percentage of sales have improved. Productivity in factory wages (the hourly workforce) increased by about 12 percent, and, among the salaried workforce in the factory, there was a 6 percent productivity gain. Even so, there is a problem with benefit costs for factory workers that we need to investigate. Year over year there has been a 35 percent reduction in scrap, so we can see that quality is improving. In fact, the manufacturing gross profit is up by 20 percent on an 11 percent increase in sales. This is all very good. The problem is that inventory was reduced in the current year and increased in the prior year. The capitalization of labor and overhead from last year's inventory buildup benefited the P&L by $4 million. This year, inventory reduction and lack of absorption for labor and overhead cost $2.4 million. This $6.4 million swing from year to year is what kept earnings flat, despite the increase in sales. And this swing is the result of noncash credits (last year) and noncash charges (this year) in order to meet generally accepted accounting principles, or GAAP.

Looking at the P&L statement this way, everything looks good. Sales are up; productivity is up; scrap is down. Materials costs are declining, and the remainder of the expenses, with the exception of factory benefits, appear to be under control. The area that most needs leadership attention is clear. More important, as shown in Figure 8.3, cash flow this year as measured by EBITDAI[3] is up 60.5 percent compared to the prior year. In addition, inventory turns are improving. This was a very good year.

Leaders looking at a company through the lens of a standard-cost P&L statement cannot see the detailed information about productivity and inventory levels, all of which has a huge impact on current and future competitiveness. They see only that sales are up and margins are down; to them, it looks like a pretty bad year. The management team has been blinded to the company's real issues. Unfortunately, their response is likely to be some form of cost cutting, which will only make matters worse.

I realize that not all companies, especially service companies, use a standard-cost system, but because these systems are so widespread

Cash Flow Statement

	This Year	Last Year	% Change
Net sales	$100,000	$90,000	11.1%
Cost of sales	(64,000)	(54,000)	18.5%
Gross profit	36,000	36,000	0.0%
SG&A	(29,000)	(27,000)	7.4%
Operating income	7,000	9,000	−22.2%
Interest expense	(1,750)	(2,000)	−12.5%
Income before taxes	5,500	7,000	−25.0%
Income taxes	(2,100)	(2,800)	−25.0%
Net income	3,150	4,200	−25.0%
Add:			
Interest	1,750	2,000	−12.5%
Income taxes	2,100	2,800	−25.0%
Depreciation	2,800	2,600	7.7%
EBITDA	9,800	11,600	−15.5%
Inventory change L/OH	2,400	(4,000)	
EBITDAI	$ 12,200	$ 7,600	60.5%

Figure 8.3 Cash Flow Statement. (Copyright 2008 by Orest J. Fiume. All rights reserved. Used with permission.)

in manufacturing companies, I think it is important to mention the problem here.

Moving to the Lean accounting model not only takes away the barrier of the traditional standard-cost system, but also helps the entire organization clearly see what is happening. Lean accounting is also less costly (requiring less financial staff) and more accurate than standard-cost accounting, as it captures only actual costs. Better information facilitates better decision making. A simplified and refocused accounting system also encourages, rather than fights, the transition to Lean.

As I mentioned earlier, despite all the pluses, you can still expect heavy resistance. More than once, I have heard CFOs insist that auditors will not accept a change from standard-cost accounting. This is not true. There is nothing in Lean accounting that violates GAAP. In every instance in which we have implemented Lean accounting, outside accountants have had no problem conducting audits and certifying financial statements.

You do not need to have completed the move to Lean accounting before your first *kaizen*. Early on, however, you should map out a plan with your CFO to eliminate standard-cost accounting within a set time frame. CFOs are conservative by nature and are not big fans of change. Expect to spend a lot of quality time talking through the merits of Lean P&L statements, for instance, and gently but firmly guiding your CFO toward more rational financial statements. The best way to demonstrate the improved visibility that the Lean P&L statement provides is to begin to prepare it in parallel with the standard-cost P&L ststement. It will not take long for the benefits to become self-evident.

While we are on the subject of accounting, as CEO, it is critical that you understand one thing about reducing inventory and GAAP. As you reduce inventory, the prior period's overhead that GAAP required you to add to inventory on the balance sheet must now be removed. There is only one place that it can go: a charge against current income. Your current income, and your earnings per share (EPS), will be penalized by these sins of the past. However, keep in mind that this is a noncash charge and that it is only a transition issue. Keep an eye on your cash flow. When inventory starts to approach 15 turns, the annual charge to earnings will become smaller and smaller until it is small enough to be ignored.

Traditional Measurements

In addition to standard-cost accounting, there are many other traditional measurements that you need to change or get rid of in order to smooth your Lean transformation. People respond to what is measured. One of my favorite examples of a bad measurement is the tendency of traditional firms to measure the relationship between direct and indirect factory workers. Over time, many people in the indirect workforce (or the work they do) are shifted to the "direct" category to beat the measurement. Meanwhile, members of the shop-floor engineering staff (who are necessary to improve the value-adding operations) fall victim to the "indirect" measurement in bad times and are laid off.

I saw a great example of this at Carrier Corporation when we were kicking off Lean. We were at one of Carrier's bigger industrial air-conditioning plants, and, after a couple of hours on the shop floor, we came back to a conference room, where I told the plant's leadership team that there was *a lot of opportunity*. Considering the mess we had just seen, I told them, we could make big improvements fast, but we needed more shop-floor engineers to implement the changes that would be required. The management team burst out laughing. They said they were not laughing at me, though. They agreed that they needed more engineers, but they had recently been forced to lay off 12 engineers because they were out of line with corporate finance's direct-to-indirect measurement. These engineers did not return, and the plant struggled to adopt Lean improvements.

Another traditional measurement problem is the fact that the standard-cost system tends to define direct labor narrowly. Only the portion of the cost that is incurred when a worker is directly touching a part is counted as direct labor. Wash-up, training, vacation, and benefit costs are thrown into an indirect or overhead category. This has the effect of hiding a major part of the direct labor costs and leads to poor decisions. One of my portfolio companies took this approach, and the managers swore up and down that their labor cost was less than 10 percent and therefore could not be lowered. When we switched to the Lean P&L statement, where we included all hourly pay and benefits in the definition, overall labor costs to make the product were actually 35 percent. This allowed the managers to think about cost reduction in a completely different way.

Also to be eliminated (or at least drastically curtailed) is the over-done, time-consuming return on investment (ROI) analysis. Do not allow your CFO to talk you into doing an ROI analysis on every *kaizen* or before equipment is moved. This is a waste of time. More important, it slows decision making and raises questions as to whether management is serious about moving to Lean. If every attempt to remove waste from the system must first be approved by accounting, the workforce will receive the message, loud and clear, that finance is in charge of determining whether it is acceptable to eliminate waste. Besides, not every Lean improvement is quantifiable by ROI. Lean works only when every associate is empowered to make improvements, as part of the team.

Tickets, Tickets, Tickets

As you move into one-piece-flow cells, you will eliminate the need for labor tickets, routings, and move tickets—all the paper that is used to track the useless trips that products and materials take around the shop floor and between functional departments. Instead, work in process will flow seamlessly from one machine or task to the next, getting value-added each time, without the need to record its motion for posterity. This will save plenty of time that direct labor personnel currently spend on a non-value-added activity, not to mention saving the salaries of finance clerks who are adding tickets and analyzing the information. There's lots of *muda* (the Japanese word for waste) here.

A great example here comes from the experience of one of my former Wiremold vice presidents. He joined a much larger electrical products manufacturer as vice president of operations after Wiremold was sold. The company had started down the Lean path and wanted to bring in some Lean expertise to help it go faster. Shortly after he arrived, however, he found that the company was adding an $80 million enterprise resource planning (ERP)[4] system to the company. The company was having major problems bringing this on line, so for his first 15 months, he was too busy scrambling to put much focus on Lean. When things settled down and he got back to Lean, he found that in one cell, where a single transaction (the arrival of a *kanban* card) had been enough to make the product before, the new ERP system had converted this into 13 separate transactions. (How's that for progress?) When he tried to change back to *kanban*, he was reminded that the company had spent $80 million on the new ERP system, and that he had to use it. He did the logical thing and quit. This is a nice story, but it is also a great example of how traditional systems can clash with Lean. If you are not close enough to your value-adding activities, you may not even be aware that this sort of foolishness is going on.

End-of-Month Financial Reviews

Soon, you will see that big month-end reviews are a form of waste and will focus your time on improving your processes. I understand, however, that this is a frightening thought. Most of us came up through the ranks in command-and-control environments, where the CEO's authority was felt most during these reviews. Can a CEO retain a hand on the helm without convening those big monthly reviews?

Closing the books at the end of the month is a necessity; I am not suggesting that you stop doing so. Some level of month-end review can even be helpful. I certainly always do this. Just make sure that these reviews are very brief and hit only the important points. The waste comes when your key people are spending three or four days a month analyzing the results and writing reports to explain what happened last month.

A Lean business is one in which leaders focus their attention on improving key process drivers—such as productivity, lead time, inventory turns, and customer service—instead of wasting time thinking about how to present the past.

Major Capital Appropriation Request Processes

The move from a traditional approach to a Lean approach is not capital-intensive. In fact, it is the opposite. *Kaizen* teams will be removing waste and improving quality with their brains instead of your wallet. Of course, shop-floor engineers will still eagerly pick up a catalog anytime someone says "process change," and in service companies, everyone wants the latest and greatest computer program, but it is your job to push consistently for creative invention instead of expensive catalog fixes.

The organization should celebrate individuals for innovation, loudly applauding every creative fix. If engineers still insist on a capital expenditure, they should be forced to do a *kaizen* event in the area several times before any capital request will be seriously considered. This is something that you want to embed into the value system of all your associates: the idea that capital spending probably represents a failure of imagination. It should certainly be your last resort, not your first.

When new spending is necessary, however, everyone should understand why the capital is needed and exactly what the company and the process will get out of it. When you arrive at this common understanding, your organization will not need a formal capital appropriation request process. If you wish to have a basis for comparing one project to another, a quick ROI calculation is all that should be required before making a decision on a *kaizen*-vetted question of capital expense. If a request document is necessary, insist that it be no more than one page in length. It should not take more than one page to demonstrate a true need.

Of course, you could stick with the traditional capital appropriation process, with all of its formality and standardized forms, analysis, and review. In a larger company, it might take six months or more to have a large capital request heard, to get a simple decision on how to spend a dollar of capital. At the same time, there is no process at all for adding millions of dollars to inventory, even though a dollar invested in inventory is the same as a dollar invested in capital equipment. I have heard the argument that the inventory dollar is variable, as opposed to the fixed capital dollar, and that is why people try to control one and not the other. I do not buy it. For most companies, inventory invariably rises over time, except when there is a big write-off. Added to that, most of the inventory that is on hand is the wrong stuff, resulting from bad forecasts or the effect of absorption accounting in production, so it is not exactly helpful in responding to customer demand. If anything should be carefully controlled, it is the inventory dollar. As CEO, you should put constant pressure on bringing down your inventory levels. Increasing inventory turns is the best indicator of whether you are making progress or not. After all, the primary reason you have a lot of inventory is to cover up all the problems that occur in your value-adding activities.

Accounting for Change

Making these key changes in the way people keep score will do more than change the numbers on the balance sheets. Taking measures such as eliminating narrow definitions of direct labor costs will greatly help your decision making and facilitate the shift to Lean instead of fighting it. These actions will drive Lean principles even more deeply into the ways people work. For example, all the excess paperwork needed to move parts from one functional department to another will go away automatically as you move to flow cells, thus lowering your costs. These changes attack some of the core tenets of your traditional approach, so it will take a consistent effort by the CEO to get them changed. Help yourself out and make sure you remove all of these obstacles.

Leveraging Lean in the Marketplace

If you begin your Lean journey with the clear objective of delivering value across the board, from suppliers to customers, you will be much more successful than if you limit Lean to just cost-cutting or inventory-lowering targets. Your Lean success will extend beyond your company walls. The way to grow your company profitably is to deliver value to your customers at a level that your competitors cannot match. Treating your vendors as your partners in delivering value to your customers is also a key part of this equation.

There is only one good reason to undergo a Lean transformation: to differentiate your organization as delivering the best value. By that, I do not mean having the lowest-cost products. In fact, Lean companies can often charge a premium for being fast, accurate, and customer-focused. Lean is about becoming the best competitor. Getting there can be a little tricky, though.

Lean offers traditional companies such fast results that instant market gratification becomes a temptation. I have seen business leaders rush to market with big promises of cheaper prices and faster turnaround after the most preliminary improvements. In the 1990s, for instance, I saw one of the biggest suppliers in the electrical industry nearly bankrupt itself by offering Lean(ish) promises from a traditional operation.

Wiremold competed with Thomas & Betts in certain areas, so we were interested observers when that company began making guarantees that certain products would always be in stock. This was a marketing promise that was made without full coordination with the company's factories, which were traditional batch operations. Soon, the factories fell behind, and the company began paying so much in fines to honor the guarantees that it had to abandon the program. Next came end-of-quarter truckload discounts followed by extended sales terms. This was a better fit with the company's traditional batch-style operations, but it had its own unique problems. If customers who ordered more than usual because of the "truckload" requirement had not sold the products at the end of the 180-day sales terms, Thomas & Betts extended the discount again, usually for another 120 days. This was effectively selling on consignment, and distributors took advantage. After a time, distributors never took Thomas & Betts's first offer, having learned that the sales force would invariably sweeten the deal. In the end, not only did the company lose money, but management got in deep trouble with the Securities and Exchange Commission for overstating revenue and earnings and had to restate several years of results. This was painful to watch and nearly put a great company out of business.

In Wiremold's case, operations were so clogged with inventory and waste in 1991 that we had to fix that before we could even think about how to strategically deliver value to our customers. Therefore, our initial focus was largely internal. As soon as operations were ready to support the drive to compete on excellence, we went to work on taking Lean to the marketplace, particularly in the areas of new products, bringing new value to the (sometimes unwilling) customers, and getting more out of our vendor relationships. Close attention to these areas backed by a Lean organization will help you move quantum leaps beyond the competition.

New Products

Perhaps the most significant way to deliver better value to your customers is through faster, more customer-centric new product development. Wiremold's product development was built upon two pillars: *kaizen* and Quality Function Deployment (QFD). A Toyota Production System method for developing new products, QFD focuses on including customer desires in product design decisions and drastically reducing time to market. Wiremold teams cut product development time by 50 to 75 percent, depending on the product type, and got into the habit of introducing two or three new products every month instead of two or three a year.

Using QFD, we incorporated the needs of the end user (including end users themselves as members of the product development team) at the design stage, to create time- and labor-saving innovations in the final product. With the voice of the customer integrated into the product design, we had more confidence entering the market and could price our products based on the value they provided instead of using the traditional cost-plus method.

For instance, our QFD teams looked at the electrical floor box category and saw opportunity. Wiremold and its competitors all made floor boxes that needed to be assembled in the field. This meant that $55-an-hour electricians were squatting on the floor, screwing a box together. Our QFD team designed a better box that could be snapped together at the job site. In fact, a contractor could install four times as many Wiremold floor boxes in an eight-hour shift as it could the competitors' product. This saved customers a lot of money and aggravation in the field, so they were happy to pay a value premium. And our distributors liked it because they benefited from the 30 percent higher-priced product, receiving more margin dollars per unit, and they were gaining market share along with Wiremold. Everybody won—except the competition, who lost market share.

As Wiremold got better at making products flow quickly through our factories, we were able to leverage the concept of configured products even further. Knowing that we could do the subassembly work four or five times faster than an electrician at a job site, we started introducing modular designs and mass customization. QFD teams created prewired raceway, custom surge strips, and wired poles, among other innovations. This allowed us to grow our market share, expand the market category, enter new markets, and expand our profit margins. A traditional batch manufacturer might have been able to mimic Wiremold's improved designs, but would have found it extremely difficult to match our mass customization because our Lean state gave us tremendous advantages.

Delivering Value to Customers

When thinking about how to bring better value to your customers, first toss out the idea that the customer is always right. The customer might be right, or he might be unconsciously sabotaging you, himself, and the entire value chain.

One of my Danaher companies, for instance, had some very large customers that were difficult to change. Jake Brake made engine retarders for heavy-duty diesel engines and sold them to the big engine and truck manufacturers. Jake Brake's factory was filled with heavy-duty equipment, running all day in batch mode and not well maintained. There was so much oil leaking onto the floor that employees spread something like a ton of absorbent material on the ground every day just to allow people to walk between the oil slicks. George K. and his team freed up about 50 percent of the total floor space in 18 months, cleaning and painting as they went. The factory went from a dark and dangerous cave to a showplace where we could bring customers. Lead times dropped from months to days. Inventory turns went from around 3 to 20. When we tried to deliver the value of short lead times and high inventory turns to our customers, however, we learned an important lesson.

This was back in the late 1980s, and Caterpillar was one of our biggest customers. We had cells dedicated to CAT products, and, as we tried to level production demand in those cells, we suggested to CAT representatives that they would benefit by ordering from us once a week instead of once a month. We talked about excess inventory, freeing up cash and space, and flexibility. They agreed. After a couple of months, however, they came back and said that their computer system could not deal with the weekly deliveries and we needed to go back to monthly.

We did as they asked, of course, but George K. and his team kept pressing the issue, going higher in the Caterpillar organization for meetings. Eventually, he got approval to go back to weekly deliveries. Then he pushed for twice weekly. By the time I left, Jake Brake was delivering CAT engine brakes three times a week and was a valuable supplier—a partner to a large and important company.

Over the years, I have seen this example repeat itself in many industries. Traditional companies tend to be compartmentalized, and the people running them assume that low inventory turns are the norm. Added to that, purchasing managers are typically measured on a cents-per-piece basis. Purchasing does not care about inventory levels. Offer a purchasing manager a $10 million reduction in inventory or a 5 percent cut in price worth $500,000 per year and the manager will take the 5 percent price cut every time. It's sad but true.

Wiremold had the same problem. We tried to convince distributors to reduce the amount of our inventory they were holding to free up their space and cash for other purposes. They could understand why this was of value, but they had a hard time actually reducing those levels. We had to show them how to do it, step by step. Our target was to increase every distributor's inventory turns of Wiremold products to 12 turns annually, from the industry's historical average of 3 or 4 turns. Then we suggested that they reinvest a portion of the freed-up cash to broaden the number of Wiremold stock-keeping units (SKUs) that they carried. In nearly every case, the broader line of Wiremold products resulted in a 10 percent sales increase and 20 percent better profitability for every distributor who did this. Even with such good results, it was hard to talk the next guy into the same program. Companies are the same as people when it comes to change.

Lower Customers' Cost of Doing Business

Over the years, companies I led have benefited from many *kaizen* events focusing on office processes that directly affected customers and distributors. I have been particularly interested in work that helped us offer better, quicker service and correspondingly lower costs of doing business. A few examples of some of these ideas on how to become more indispensable to your customer while strengthening your own Lean organization are:

- Lower customer costs by improving direct interfaces.
- Turn around all quotes in a single day.
- Answer the phone within three rings, with no abandoned calls.
- Eliminate errors from order entry through shipment.

Creating a system in which every telephone call is answered within three rings might take a single *kaizen* event, or it might take three. Some problems will be more stubborn than others. The trick is to keep going back to problem areas until you achieve the results you need.

For instance, Wiremold had both off-the-shelf products and a custom business that required detailed quotes. Custom work was about 35 percent of our business. At Walker Systems, the under-floor duct business was more custom than standard, and associates quoted jobs off blueprints. Walker's quoting department was large, and each quote went into a lot of detail; associates often took 10 to 14 days to turn a quote around. We were losing business because of the lag, but it could not be done faster, according to the leaders of the quote department. We did a number of *kaizen* projects on this, including the vice president of sales and the vice president of marketing on the teams. We eliminated the step of creating detailed drawings with each quote, and we allowed quotes to have a plus-or-minus 3 percent range of accuracy instead of claiming to be accurate to the penny. In the end, we were turning quotes around in a single day. Sales grew and costs fell, particularly for our customers. Walker Systems became a trusted partner instead of just another hurdle that the customer had to jump through.

Better Ordering Practices

Just like everyone else in your organization, salespeople need to change the way they perceive and accomplish their jobs. In the past, order entry and inside sales associates were trained to fulfill what the customer *said* was needed, without question. What we discovered, however, was that our customers were often using bad practices that could easily derail our own Lean journey. So, one of the early changes we made was to have all inside sales associates follow two key guidelines:

1. Never tell a customer the quantity of a product we have in stock.
2. Never sell more than 80 percent of the stock on hand to a single customer.

Prior to Lean, our customers were in the habit of calling to say that they needed floor boxes, for instance, and asking how many we had in stock. The customer service representative might consult a computer and say, "We have 800." If the customer was calling to order supplies for the next 90 days—a common practice—and needed 1,000 of those electrical boxes designed to be sunk in a floor, he might respond, "OK, send me the 800 boxes now and let me know when the other 200 will be ready."

At this point, Wiremold would be out of stock on a popular item and might have to back-order the next 50 customers, and this customer would be making room for 800 floor boxes that he did not need immediately. The electrical contractor in this case needed no more than 90 boxes a week to complete his jobs, but his ordering habits made us run out of stock and cost him money—largely in warehousing costs, plus the risk of lost or damaged product. In addition, if a project stalled or was cancelled, the contractor would have useless inventory. The better solution would be for Wiremold to set up a weekly schedule, delivering the boxes needed directly to the job site.

So, in response to questions about stock on hand, we trained sales associates to never give a numeric answer, but instead to ask about the quantity needed and the work schedules, to get a better understanding of how the product was being used and at what frequency. Then we could set up product deliveries that made sense for the customer, without inconveniencing the rest of our customers with back orders. It amazes me to this day that companies adopt a mantra of being customer-driven, without recognizing that they are sometimes being driven off a cliff. They give the customer what is requested, back-order everyone else for three weeks, and try to solve the problem by increasing inventory levels for that product.

Level Incoming Demand

Most of what causes lumpy incoming order patterns originates within your own company. Eliminating your own bad behavior will help level the flow of orders and, by extension, help level out production. Consider doing the following, by *kaizen* or by policy decision:

- Rewrite sales terms that encourage customers to order 40 to 50 percent of the monthly demand in the final week of a month.
- Eliminate loader programs.
- Review promotional programs with an eye to leveling orders.
- Do not give volume discounts.
- Work with customers to eliminate big batch orders.
- Avoid all stupid sales tricks intended to make the month or the quarter.

For service companies, try not to stimulate demand that is beyond your capacity to handle in a reasonable time. Hospital demand is a bit random, but freeing up beds as early in the day as possible will allow for a smoother flow and enhanced revenue opportunities.

Attack these issues one at a time, starting with the ones that are creating the most order fluctuation. At Wiremold, it was our sales terms. Manufacturers in the electrical industry all had essentially the same sales terms. If you ordered by the twenty-fifth of the month and paid by the tenth day of the second month, you could take a 2 percent discount. For example, if you placed an order on May 25 and paid by July 10, you got 2 percent off the total cost of the order. Because the average electrical distributor makes just 2 to 3 percent pretax profit, this 2 percent discount had the effect of forcing 40 to 50 percent of our incoming orders—and corresponding shipments—into the last week of the month. This was a definite barrier to our attempts to level-load production and deliver better value to our customers.

Early in Wiremold's Lean conversion, I told Scott Bartosch, our vice president of sales, that we needed to change our sales terms so that distributors paid us twice per month. If looks could kill, I would be dead. Scott was one of the best sales managers in the entire electrical industry and a good businessperson, so he understood how sales terms could interfere with production demand and our goals for customer service. But he was not happy with the prospect of telling customers to pay us twice a month. And yes, the new sales terms created some unhappy distributors who did not want to change their routines, even with the promise of future value. It took about two years of steady talking to get everyone changed over, but it did happen—helping Wiremold to become a more reliable provider, and our distributors to make more profit from our products.

A change in sales terms alone did not flatten demand completely, of course. Distributors relied on material resource planning (MRP) systems to tell them when to reorder and how much, and those MRP systems had everyone ordering three months' worth of product at a time. So, we kept looking for ways to change the tide. We eliminated the loader programs that were prevalent in our industry. We taught our sales force to get strict, allowing distributors to carry only the amount of inventory that was suitable to the market, which we defined based on conditions in a particular market. If a distributor placed an order that was too large for his market or business, we would refuse it. Sometimes a distributor was shocked when we said no. None of the other manufacturers behaved like that; they loved big orders. After explaining our rationale, however, we were always able to reach an agreement. More than one distributor came back later and thanked us for opening their eyes and preventing those big product returns that were expensive for both companies.

We also held fast to a single price-into-stock policy, no matter what the size of the order or the distributor. All of our competitors were more than happy to give volume discounts, of course, so this upset some of our distributors. But we held fast and kept explaining our position: everyone gets the same price into stock, no matter how big or small the distributor. We did, however, offer a rebate for distributors based on annual volume, loyalty to our products, and the distributor's growth for the year. That was fine with distributors, as long as there was a level playing field regarding price into stock. It also helped to stabilize the price for Wiremold products in the market, since volume discounts usually found their way back into the marketplace, whereas annual volume, growth, and loyalty payments did not. Everybody won.

Early on, we also created a program called Cycle Truck to deliver products to our larger distributors. Each truck had a set route, and the number of stops it made depended on the size of the customers on the route. For instance, a truck might come every Thursday morning, and we could promise that anything that was ordered by noon on Tuesday of that week would be on the regular weekly truck. Distributors loved the reliability, and the Cycle Trucks helped to level out orders even more.

Our big vision was to ultimately wean distributors off their MRP systems and have them just tell us what they sold every day. Within certain parameters, we could treat daily sales information as an order and put it on the weekly Cycle Truck. Because we delivered 52 times per year, distributors could drop their inventory to two or three weeks' instead of three or four months' worth and still be fully in stock. Wiremold would have a smooth demand pattern, and our customers would have more space, more cash, and fewer inventory headaches. It would be very hard for them to displace us as their vendor.

Leverage Your Customer's Measurements

If you sell through distributors or to large retailers, you should be able to utilize those companies' measurement systems to your advantage. As most retailers operate on tight margins and buy from a variety of manufacturers, they are interested in determining what type of return they get from each manufacturer.

In the electrical industry, most distributors belonged to the National Association of Electrical Distributors, and they used GMROI (gross margin return on investment) to measure vendors. Because inventory is their principal investment, the actual calculation is:

$$\text{GMROI} = \frac{\text{gross profit on sales of stocked products}}{\text{average inventory dollars}}$$

The lower your GMROI, the worse you looked as a vendor. If you had service or quality problems and had a low GMROI, then you really took some heat. And, as you might expect from someone running a low-margin (2 to 3 percent pretax) distribution business, GMROI was used all the time to beat up producers on price.

For instance, let's say a distributor stocks your product and sells $1 million annually. He makes a 25 percent gross margin on these sales, or $250,000 per year. Improving your GMROI by increasing the gross margin on these sales is very difficult. If you drop the price by 5 percent, most distributors will just see this as an opportunity to pass the price savings along to customers to gain market share against other similar distributors. Distributors almost never hang on to a price reduction. Their internal pricing mechanism targets a 25 percent gross margin, and they are either content with that or simply do not believe that they can get a higher margin.

You can, however, leverage your GMROI score significantly by working on the denominator of the equation. For example, let's look at the impact of various inventory turn levels on GMROI in Table 9.1.

Table 9.1 Leveraging Your GMROI Score
$1 million in sales @ 25% gross margin

Inventory Turns	Inventory $		GMROI
3	$330,000	=	0.75 GMROI
4	$250,000	=	1.00 GMROI
10	$100,000	=	2.50 GMROI

By reducing setup and lead times and introducing pull systems, producers can deliver real value. In this example, by taking distributor inventory turns from three times to ten times annually, you gave that distributor $230,000 in cash to invest in his business or put in his pocket. Unlike a 5 percent price cut, which goes straight to the market in the form of lower prices, this is cash that the distributor can keep. It is a rare windfall. At the same time, you have more than tripled your GMROI score. You are no longer in the middle of the pack; you are now one of his top five vendors. Now, you have more to talk about than price alone, because there are steps that both organizations can take next to leverage Lean and strategically increase your market share with end users.

In Wiremold's case, we focused on getting distributors to reinvest a portion of that liberated cash into a much broader array of our products. We wanted distributors to have the breadth of Wiremold products and to rely on our rapid replenishment capabilities for depth of inventory. Those distributors who had inventory turning at least 10 times saw the benefits. They became known in local markets for always having the odd Wiremold parts in stock, and this helped them grow their overall sales, since most customers simply bought all their Wiremold parts in one place. Some other local Wiremold distributors would even use our high-turning distributors as their source for the odd low-volume parts. In this way, Wiremold was able to grow the business at higher prices, while still giving significant amounts of cash back to our channel partners.

For hospitals and service companies whose customers wouldn't normally measure something like GMROI, think about focusing on something that they would measure. For example, most hospitals measure patient satisfaction, and most service companies have some measure of what their customers think of them. Improving the processes that will lever this customer satisfaction should be a key focus of your Lean efforts.

Speed Kills (the Competition)

For companies that sell direct to end users and for custom job-shop operations, one of the best ways to leverage Lean is to focus on cutting the time for everything you do. If you can turn a quote around in a day and your competitors take two to three weeks, you have a big advantage. Similarly, if your lead time from order to ship is one week, while the competition takes six weeks, you will gain market share. In fact, Lean offers even more advantage for custom businesses than it does for standard product businesses—a fact that is often misunderstood by custom manufacturers.

Abbreviating time to market can save money for customers, as well. Years ago, I was a director of a small jewelry (rings) manufacturer near Miami whose biggest customer was J. C. Penney. This was a traditional shop that would make 100 identical rings at a time and carried a lot of inventory (inventory turns were in the range of 2 to 3 times). The lead time to make a batch of 100 rings was eight weeks.

The CEO asked me to come in and help. I started by creating a flow cell and got them making rings based on incoming orders, instead of one big batch of identical rings. The flow cell—responsible for all J. C. Penney orders, of course—was staffed by ten middle-aged women who spoke only Spanish and three male stone setters. Their goal was to make 275 rings per day. We set up a production control board[1] to keep track and posted the results every hour where everyone could see it. For the first month, we could not hit the target, but we kept fixing problems as they occurred. Finally, one day a cheer went up in the factory: the team had beaten the 275 target. They then started beating each new number until they were producing 450 rings per day with the same 13 people. There was no financial incentive for the associates here, just the personal challenge of beating the daily target and setting a new record.

So, we increased productivity by 64 percent, but here was the real game changer: the lead time dropped from eight weeks to two days. Every order that came in could be waxed up today and shipped tomorrow. Rings were still made in batches of 100, but they were all of different designs corresponding to the orders that had come in that day from J. C. Penney. The factory no longer had to carry much more than a day's worth of inventory and could smooth out the cyclical nature of the business. The customer did not need to buy in big batches far in advance, allowing the store to react more quickly to fashion trends and largely eliminate its need to return excess or unsold goods. The springtime parade of obsolete inventory being returned went away, along with the customer's need to finance extra inventory.

Another valuable approach for custom-order and service companies is to arrange *kaizen* events with customers to reduce the amount of lead time and errors that occur in the daily interface. As an example, one of my portfolio companies is in the printing business. When it did a *kaizen* on its customer service complaints, it found that more than 60 percent had nothing to do with the actual printing. Instead, the complaints were about order entry errors, shipping errors, pricing errors, problems with the up-front artwork coming from the customers, and a list of other issues, all surrounding the customer interface. Bringing in your bigger customers for a one-week joint *kaizen* can help eliminate these errors and make you a more valuable supplier.

Delivering Value to Vendors

The power structure in most value chains is primitive at best. Customers make demands on producers; producers demand better terms from vendors. It is likely that you maintain several vendors for the same parts, just to play one off against the others and squeeze a little better price. And in your purchasing department, people have been taught to think only in terms of cents each. They will buy a six months' supply of something to get a few percentage points off the price. The cost of carrying this inventory—moving it, storing it, and the risk of obsolescence—is never factored into the calculations.

Lean companies take a different approach. They are always looking to assess the total cost of doing business. You will want daily deliveries from all your vendors, for instance, in order to keep production running smoothly, without excess inventory. But you cannot browbeat your vendors into doing your will. They must be taught to see the waste of inventory and the benefit of being your valued partner.

At Wiremold, we had three local suppliers of cardboard boxes—all of them reluctant to deliver daily. We offered 100 percent of our business to the first of these suppliers that was willing to try daily deliveries. To help that supplier, we sent *kaizen* teams to his plant to show his employees how to reduce setup times and to help them establish a *kanban* system. The supplier was happy because he saw how he could deliver value to his other customers, too, using these methods. And both of us were saving money.

In no time, the other two vendors were back pounding at our door, offering daily deliveries—now that they knew we were serious—for even less cost than before. But we had saved our new partner-supplier so much money in his business that he was already giving us a better price.

Over the course of about four years at Wiremold, we went from 340 vendors down to just 42—all of them delivering daily. In fact, our largest vendor was about six hours away in Baltimore, and that company was still able to deliver six to eight truckloads of steel to our factory in Hartford every day. Instead of tripping over a four-month supply of steel (our pre-*kaizen* state), we had one or two days' worth on hand and better customer service, besides. With 42 vendors instead of 340, we did not need that separate purchasing silo, either, and we could integrate those associates into other parts of the business. This saved us a lot of money.

As you can see, all these initiatives save money both for us and for our partners. The next question is: how do we continue to build on these gains?

The Coming-Back Fee

This is the fun part. For those Lean leaders who can overcome the hurdles and implement Lean, a new world of strategic possibilities opens. Not only can you leverage the turnaround speed that comes from your new Lean state, but you can also leverage your quality and customer service capabilities.

A great example of this comes from my days as group executive for the Danaher Corporation. One of the businesses in my group made Swiss screw machine parts for various original equipment manufacturers (OEMs). These were turned parts, and they were usually components in a larger assembly. The Swiss screw machine industry is characterized by many small, local operations. It is an easy market to enter and therefore is very competitive. The average pretax margin in the industry is less than 5 percent.

A Danaher company, the Isley Corporation, was one of the largest players in the market and made more than 30 percent margin pretax. This was not due to its size or scale, but was because we had a terrific leader running the business, Ugi Lighting. Ugi was a strong-minded leader who had worked in the industry for decades. He kept his team members efficient; they had a quick turnaround and would jump through hoops to make sure that customers got parts on time, even when the customers forgot to order on time or in the right amount. Isley was not always the lowest-cost competitor; it competed on operational excellence. Ugi was able to maintain that big pretax margin through efficiency and the fact that customers were willing to pay for high quality and the knowledge that they would get their parts on time.

Of course, with so many small competitors who were willing to take work at low margins, it should come as no surprise that Ugi's customers could usually go down the street and get an individual part quoted for something like 20 percent less. Whenever this happened, Ugi would acknowledge the fact that someone might be able to quote 20 percent less, but he would hold fast on price. The customer might be reminded of Isley's quality, and maybe of the time he had been bailed out of a jam by Ugi's quick response. Mostly, the customers were convinced to stay.

Once in a while, however, the customer would walk away in search of that 20 percent off. At that point, all Ugi could do was thank the customer for past business and say that he would still be there should the customer be disappointed by the competition. Then the customer was told how much it would cost him to leave and come back. You see, Ugi was able to charge a 20 percent coming-back fee. That 20 percent would be tacked onto every order for the first year that the customer was back, itemized on the invoice under "coming-back fee." It was amazing how many customers came back and paid that fee because, in the final analysis, it was cheaper to pay the extra charge for a year than have assembly lines shut down for lack of a 25-cent part.

Can you imagine that in your own industry—a company so excellent that it could charge customers extra to come back after a dalliance with a low-cost competitor? This is a good target for any company that is undergoing a Lean turnaround. When you hit bumps in the road, or when you have to explain why Lean will work for the fiftieth time, think about that coming-back fee.

It is possible even for your company.

Capitalizing on Your Gains

Turning your company around using Lean will rapidly improve your earnings, cash flow, and enterprise value. Allowing all your associates to share in the gains will allow you to improve even faster and get you to the stage where you have a Lean culture even quicker. For senior managers, make sure that the bonus plan has some stretch goals and that it weights earnings and working capital equally in order to give you the biggest gain in enterprise value. Focus your own attention on the shop floor, and make sure that you actualize your gains and that you take all the "leaps of faith" that your Lean transformation will present to you.

These gains will create the foundation for even greater success. As your Lean journey progresses, capitalize on the advantages that Lean gives you in acquisitions, providing the cash and the game plan and lowering the risks. Establish your own standard work for acquisitions and not only will your cash come back to you quickly, but the new acquisition will soon be generating excess cash that you can use to buy more companies.

The transformation from a traditional to a Lean enterprise will provide a lot of opportunities. Your lead times will shrink, and you will be much more responsive to your customers. Quality and productivity will improve dramatically, and you will be a stronger competitor. Inventory will drop, space will be freed up, and you will have more cash on hand. Oh, and of course you will gain market share and grow, and your earnings will go up.

All of this sounds very nice, but the question is: how do you as CEO make sure that all this happens and, more important, how do you leverage your gains? You're going to have higher earnings and more cash; how do you use this to your advantage? Well, let's start with your people. Adopting a Lean strategy is all about people. You are trying to transform your people. It follows, then, that how you reward them and the incentives you give them should be among your top priorities. Start with the understanding that moving to Lean is a team sport. You need everyone's participation and ideas if you are to be successful. As a result, any wealth that is created should be shared in some way with all your associates. So let's begin there, and later in this chapter we can talk about what to do with the excess cash you will be generating.

Profit Sharing

As you convert to Lean, your company will eventually be able to produce its current volume with 25 to 40 percent fewer people than it needs now. This will give you plenty of room in the budget to share the gains of Lean with your people. After all, most of the best ideas on how to eliminate the waste will come from the people who are doing the work.

My recommendation is that you establish a profit-sharing program in which every employee participates on an equal footing. It should be based on the company's actual earnings, as opposed to the annual budget, and it should pay out from the first dollar of profit. In other words, if the company makes a profit, that profit is shared. No profit, no payment. A good profit-sharing program also pays out at least once per quarter. A monthly payout is even better to keep the company's progress top of mind for all employees.

Stay away from complicated gain-sharing formulas or plans that pay out only above a target level that keeps moving up. This will inevitably make it look as if the company is trying to game the system, and employees will not believe that management is serious about including them in the company's gains.

The best profit-sharing plan I have come across was the one that was in place at Wiremold, developed in 1916 by the company's founder, D. Hayes Murphy.

Wiremold Profit-Sharing Plan

$$\frac{15\% \text{ of pretax earnings}}{\text{Total straight-time wages}} = \text{profit-sharing percentage}$$

Profit-sharing percentage $\times$ individual's straight-time wages for the quarter = profit-sharing check

---

Wiremold paid out on the profit-sharing plan once per quarter, although we posted results once a month. Along with the check, employees were required to attend a brief quarterly profit-sharing meeting that I conducted. At remote business sites, the quarterly meetings were conducted by division presidents. Usually the meeting lasted no more than 20 minutes, during which time we shared financial and Lean results, plus improvement plans for the next quarter to increase profit sharing. We then opened up the meeting for questions so that all associates could participate. This drove home the point that everyone in the company was tied together and that all were enriched by Lean work. Much of the talk focused on customer demand, but we also used this conversation as a forum for quashing rumors, talking about what we would focus on in the coming quarter, and ensuring that everyone heard the same message. After we began our Lean journey, Wiremold's people paid even closer attention to the profit-sharing results, wanting to know what they could do to help improve their percentage. When the profit-sharing percentage rose from a 1 to 2 percent payout before *kaizen* to in excess of 10 percent with a few quarters near 20 percent, we had everyone's full commitment.

The Lean Management Incentive System

In addition to having a companywide profit-sharing plan, you will also need a management incentive system supporting the Lean transformation. This is not unlike the traditional bonus plan that most companies have in place to attract and retain the highest-quality management team, which is necessary for competitive reasons, but it is structured differently in a Lean company. For example, bonuses for the whole management team should be paid solely based upon how the company did against its goals. There should be no personal component to the company performance bonus, as that would have a negative impact on the teamwork needed to make the Lean conversion. Save personal recognition for an individual's salary increase, or for the way stock options are awarded. For example, if the company achieved 80 percent of its bonus target, everyone in the bonus pool has his own bonus target percentage multiplied by 80 percent to determine the individual's annual bonus.

Here are the three components of my recommended bonus pool and how the pool is divided:

Optimal Bonus Structure for Lean	
Operating earnings	40%
Working capital turns	40%
Strategic objectives	20%
Total	100%

Using equal weights for earnings and working capital turns is important for a Lean company. Remember that inventory hides waste. Therefore, inventory reduction is key to removing waste and encouraging value to flow. In fact, I would argue that what you do to increase inventory and working capital turns[1] is exactly what will drive up your earnings. High inventory turns are the hallmark of companies with good quality, strong productivity, low scrap, less space, shorter lead times, and other such advantages. Improving the working capital items on your balance sheet is what enables the company to deliver value to your customer, which in turn drives earnings. More important, focusing on both earnings and working capital turns equally will create the biggest gain in enterprise value—something, by the way, that we are keenly aware of in the private-equity world.

This structure for the management bonus pool helps everyone focus on the balance sheet—something that is regrettably ignored in most companies. Not only do balance sheet improvements drive earnings, but they also drive cash flow. In recession years, like 2009, most companies cannot meet their original earnings' goals because of market declines that are beyond their control. Companies can, however, still deliver good cash flow by focusing on improving their working capital turns. The management team can still get 60 percent or more of the bonus target this way, even when the payout for earnings is zero.

One of my portfolio companies is an excellent example here. From the first day of 2009, the global recession was in full evidence, and sales dropped steadily, finishing off the year 21 percent below the company's 2008 totals. Earnings before interest, taxes, depreciation, and amortization (EBITDA) was down 24 percent, so there was no way the management team could make its full goals in the earnings column—even though the managers had responded well and used Lean to beat both budgeted earnings and the prior year in each of the last six months of the year. Instead, they focused on working capital and cash flow to beat their targets, thus giving everyone a reasonable bonus payout. Table 10.1 shows the results.

Working capital turns improved by 14 percent, from 7.1 times to 8.1 times, and as a result, senior staff members exceeded their budget goal for working capital turns (7.4 times) and got a payout of about 54 percent on the working capital part of their plan. They received a full payout on the strategic part of their plan (20 percent) and achieved 82 percent of their bonus payout despite missing most of the earnings

Table 10.1   Portfolio Company E
Years ended December 31 ($ in millions)

	2009	2008	% Change
Accounts receivable	$126.9	$150.3	−16%
+ Inventory	47.9	78.6	−39%
− Accounts payable	66.6	67.9	−2%
Working capital	108.2	161.0	−33%

targets in the plan. Still, this worked for the overall business goals because cash more than doubled (+102 percent) and we had a debt-free company with $114 million of cash. In addition, this company's cumulative Lean efforts increased both gross margins and EBITDA margins, despite the 21 percent decline in sales. The year-end balance sheet also showed inventories lower than trade payables. Suppliers were, in effect, financing the company. More important, lead times were short and customer service was very good, allowing the company to outperform the competition and collect premium prices in a commodity market.

Without a bonus structure that gave the same weight to working capital turns and earnings, this would not have happened. Build incentives into your balance sheet. It pays off.

Also, limit strategic objectives—which account for 20 percent of the bonus structure—to only four to six key strategic items that will truly enhance your ability to deliver value to your customers. Objectives such as increasing customer service, introducing new products, improving quality, reductions in lead time, entering new markets, installing a new computer system, or consolidating a factory are good examples here. These should be tough goals, not easy layups.

Actualize Your Gains

Another critical lesson I have learned over the years is that every company needs to actualize its improvements. This is easy to overlook—particularly if you are a person who likes to go out and take immediate action, but is not so good at the follow-up—but it is important for the whole organization's understanding of Lean.

For example, if *kaizen* teams working under a no-layoff policy have freed 10 people from a work area, you now must reassign those people to a different area in order for the gains to be realized and for the benefit to hit your P&L. In the best-case scenario, growth within the company enables those 10 people to be absorbed easily. If you do not have rapid growth, but you do have temporary employees or a lot of overtime, increased productivity in one area can be used to reduce the number of temporary employees or excessive work hours in another—a move that still allows you to actualize your gains. Or, consider putting the most capable of your newly freed employees into the *kaizen* promotion office (KPO) to help generate additional improvements and speed the company's transformation, or use these employees to insource work that is currently sent to outside companies. Whatever your solution, make sure that it is carried out so that everyone can see that the changes that have been made have improved profit sharing and are permanent.

Acquisitions

Now let's deal with how to use the cash that you will be freeing up. Your strategy statement will need a growth section to absorb excess space and people, part of which (as was the case with Wiremold) might include acquisitions. If that's the case, you will find that Lean provides you with three distinct advantages. Lean:

- Provides the cash.
- Lowers the risks.
- Creates a clear game plan to follow.

Let's look more closely at each of these points.

Provides the Cash

When I joined Wiremold in September 1991, the company had low earnings and very little cash. But the way I saw it, there was money lying around everywhere in the form of excess people and inventory. All we needed was to get organized and use Lean to pick it all up. The most dramatic results at Wiremold came in the form of inventory reduction. After two years of focused Lean work, our inventory turns went from 3.4 times annually at the end of 1990 to 10 times annually at the end of 1993.

When inventory turned quickly, it was no longer getting stacked up everywhere. During this time, we managed to free up about 50 percent of our factory floor space. Also, we were able to reduce excess inventory to the tune of $11.2 million. If we use 10 percent as a carrying cost, it would have cost $1.1 million per year just to have this inventory sit around gathering dust.

Using Inventory Reduction to Finance Acquisitions	
1993 inventory at 1990 turn rate	$16.7 million
Less actual 1993 inventory	$5.6 million
Cash freed up	$11.1 million

We used this cash to do five small acquisitions in 1993 that were designed to increase our product portfolio. For instance, one company that Wiremold purchased made metal raceway that was prewired for electrical use, and we wanted to fold that company into ours. We now had the floor space to devote to another product, and we knew how to reduce the footprint of that business so that it would fit into a small space. In total, these five acquisitions cost $10 million and contributed $24 million in annual sales, producing a 10 percent pretax profit, or $2.4 million, instead of saddling us with that $1.1 million in inventory carrying costs. This was a huge gain for us, and it all came from putting our waste to work, so to speak. We woke up the "sleeping money" that others call inventory.

Lowers the Risks

Any acquisition brings a certain amount of risk. Approaching a purchase target with a Lean set of eyes, however, helps you see possibilities that others do not, allowing you to bid a little higher than the competition to make the deal.

For example, let's say you are considering a small acquisition that you can tuck into your current operations. The target has $3 million in inventory and just three annual inventory turns. You know you can improve inventory turns to ten times or better in pretty short order, which gives you a strategic advantage. At ten annual inventory turns, you get $2.1 million of your purchase price back in cash in just a few years. A company this small—let's say it has $12.8 million in sales and $1.2 million in EBITDA—might cost about $6 to $7 million. Lowering inventory by $2.1 million would get you one-third of your purchase price within about two years, giving you a great safety cushion. Cutting inventory will also reduce floor space by 50 percent or more. This might allow you to consolidate this acquisition into an existing facility, saving about $200,000 per year in rent, taxes, and other overhead costs. In addition, you should be able to increase productivity and grow the earnings margin by 3 to 5 points over the first two years. At the low end of this range, you will add $400,000 per year to EBITDA. This, combined with the inventory reduction, overhead savings from space reduction, and the base EBITDA of $1.2 million per year, should allow you to get your entire purchase price back in cash in three years or less. If you can grow the target company's sales at the same time, your cash will come back even faster.

In my experience, traditional companies with low sales growth— between 1 and 3 percent—or even slight sales declines can achieve about 10 percent annual internal sales growth once the benefits of Lean are realized (through shorter lead times, better customer service, and fewer defects). This capacity to grow provides another layer of protection when making acquisitions as a Lean executive. Most companies can add the target company's products to their portfolio or utilize the acquired company's sales channels to open new markets for even more leverage.

Creates a Clear Game Plan to Follow

How many times have you seen one company purchase another and have it result in more confusion than profit? In some companies, every time an acquisition is made, the wheel needs to be invented all over again. Staff members might take the first six months studying the new acquisition's operations, sales, and customer service before making any decisions, leaving the acquisition's management flailing anxiously.

If Lean is your strategy, however, from the moment you arrive, you know what needs to be done and how. On the day the sale is official, the CEO should be onsite, kicking off the acquisition's Lean transformation. There is no need to study the business's current practices; they are about to be changed, anyway. Inform the new company of your Lean strategy and start the training immediately.

At Wiremold, we had standard work for new acquisitions. I always made the first visit to a newly acquired company, spoke to all the employees in person, if possible, and gave a little overview of Wiremold. Being part of Wiremold meant that all employees were now part of our profit-sharing program, and I explained that our target was to make profit sharing equal to 20 percent of base pay. Now that all the employees knew that they had skin in the game, they were usually more receptive to our improvement ideas.

After the overview, we launched right into a two- or three-hour Lean training session. I conducted this session as well, illustrating Lean principles, outlining what we expected from team members, and explaining how we would help them meet those expectations. The fact that I did the introduction and training sent the message that Lean was a core value at Wiremold, and that any foot-dragging, wait-and-see attitudes among new associates would be frowned upon.

The first *kaizen* improvement projects started the very first day. We picked the areas in which to work, formed a couple of teams led by me and other Wiremold Lean experts, and got started. By the end of the first or second day, we would be moving machines and creating a new flow layout on the shop floor. This was usually a shock for the new associates. Some of those machines had not been moved in 20 years or more. By the end of the week, we had always freed up floor space, reduced inventory and lead times on some key product lines, and achieved significant productivity gains. We knew that this would happen every time because we knew the power of Lean. And it was impossible for new associates to come away from this first week thinking that we were not serious about Lean. This was our intent, of course. Before leaving, we always scheduled the next several *kaizen* events to avoid losing momentum.

During this first week, the members of our finance team were also working with their new counterparts to transfer the financial processes over to our monthly reporting package. This was a move away from standard-cost accounting to Lean accounting—a critical move for new companies that remained somewhat independent, but would still be part of the Wiremold family. Any company that was using standard-cost accounting was, in effect, placing a high value on the inventory that was clogging its systems, giving the impression that inventory created wealth. A few chief financial officers displayed withdrawal symptoms upon losing their old standard-cost system, but most found logic in the statement that productivity, not inventory, creates wealth.

Sales and marketing teams were also brought in early, particularly if we had just acquired a smaller competitor or a business with complementary products that would be sold through our existing distribution channels. Unless we were very careful about timing the announcement of a company purchase, distributors would jump the gun, ordering not-yet-integrated products on Wiremold order forms under Wiremold sales terms. In Wiremold's market channel, sales were often a complicated patchwork of direct employees and sales representative agencies, and we always needed a little extra time to straighten out the situation. Therefore, we learned to have sales and marketing teams with us on day one of an acquisition. Still, there was occasional confusion and employee overlap. One independent sales representative, for instance, was found to be superfluous during an early acquisition. He quickly found another competitor to represent, but then Wiremold bought this new company, where he was also deemed redundant. By the time we bought a third company that he represented, he called us to resign before the acquisition was even complete.

Lean Acquisition Examples

Even companies that are already working on improvement programs can be substantially enriched with Lean. Brooks Electrics, for example, which Wiremold acquired about three years before I arrived, had been following the total quality teachings of W. Edwards Deming and was the most forward-thinking operation in Wiremold by the early 1990s. The company was housed in a rather awkward two-level building in an older industrial section of Philadelphia. We got the company started on Lean in early 1992 when Gary Brooks, who had founded the business with his father, was still running the show. He was a good manager, and he was very open to new ideas and to Lean thinking.

After beginning the transformation, Brooks's improvement teams reduced inventory quickly and freed up valuable floor space, allowing us to consolidate a couple of small acquisitions into the Brooks facility. This created some disruption in 1993 and even into 1994, but once the dust settled, Brooks was able to post some impressive results, as shown in Table 10.2.

Table 10.2 Brooks Electronics Results 1993–1998 ($ in millions)

	1993	1998	% Change
Sales	$14.8	$23.3	+ 57%
Operating income	$(0.7)	$4.8	N/A
Sales per employee	$98,000	$167,000	+ 70%
Inventory turns	4.1×	27.9×	+580%
Working capital turns	6.5×	16.4×	+152%

With this type of performance, Brooks was capable of funding its own growth, plus contributing excess cash to finance additional Wiremold acquisitions. This was a critical success. Often, companies make acquisitions, only to find that the new businesses are a big cash drain for the parent company for several years, piling additional cost onto the price paid for the acquisition in the first place. By implementing Lean, Brooks became a cash-positive acquisition for Wiremold that enabled us to continue to buy other companies.

While the fundamental Lean principles were behind the transition at Brooks, it would not have happened without true leadership at the top. Gary Brooks understood and embraced Lean and put his own energy behind the transformation. Gary, by the way, went on to run Wiremold when I retired in 2002 and today is the CEO of Esselte Corporation, one of the world's largest manufacturers of filing products and one of my portfolio companies.

Another acquisition that demonstrates Lean's advantages was a smaller product line acquisition from 1995, Raceway Components, Inc (RCI), which made fire-rated, poke-through floor boxes (electrical outlets). It was a stand-alone business located in New Jersey with a union workforce, the IBEW. RCI was a great fit for Wiremold's Walker Systems business, located in West Virginia, an industry leader in under-floor ductwork and electrical floor boxes. At the time of the acquisition, however, Walker was just beginning the move away from an old, inefficient building to a new location about 10 miles away. We knew that RCI would eventually be a good fit for Walker, but we had no place to put it, really. Therefore, we used *kaizen* improvement projects on the New Jersey plant first and put off the decision as to whether we should consolidate this acquisition with Walker in West Virginia.

As always with a new acquisition, I led the early *kaizen* projects in New Jersey. The shop-floor team and the IBEW associates were a lot of fun; there were laughs and funny stories coming out of every *kaizen* event. At the same time, these were serious improvement projects, and we made rapid progress. In the first year, we freed up more than half of the floor space and more than doubled inventory turns. Customer service got better, and sales grew. When the time came to make the decision on what to do with this plant, it was very difficult. We liked the people, and they had done a great job. Even so, the economics were overwhelmingly in favor of moving the operation to West Virginia.

The fact that we already had production moving through cells by product families made the move easier. One complete value stream at a time could be picked up, with all its equipment, and moved to West Virginia without disrupting other value streams. This allowed the move to proceed at a measured pace and significantly lowered the normal risks. We could tell the receiving plant exactly how many square feet were needed, avoiding the typical problem of reconfiguring equipment layouts in a new facility. RCI more than paid back its purchase price in less than three years and then became a significant cash contributor to Wiremold's future growth. Because we had always been up front about the fact that we would consolidate this business with another, it came as no surprise to the employees. However, the gains made by RCI employees allowed us to treat them very generously at the end. Some sample results are given in Table 10.3.

A third example was the wiring products division of Dual Light in Idaho. Its product line fit with that of a Wiremold division located outside of Los Angeles, Airey-Thompson, Inc., which made specialty wire management and lighting. As in the West Virginia case, the California

Table 10.3   RCI—the Wiremold Company 1995–1998
($ in millions)

	1995	1998	% Change
Sales	$6	$14	+133%
Head count	44	15	− 66%
Square feet	50,000	4,000	− 92%
Inventory turns	2.5×	12.0×	+380%
Inventory dollars	$1.3	$0.3	− 77%

division was in the process of moving to a new facility at the time, so we went into the acquisition not knowing when we would be able to consolidate the two businesses. We started *kaizen* work at the Idaho facility immediately, knowing that we would need improvements quickly, since this particular product line had lost money for five years in a row under its prior owners.

The acquisition closed on a Monday. On Tuesday morning, the president of our California businesses, Bob Ahlstrom, and I arrived at our new company. We introduced ourselves to the members of the management team and gave them a little overview. Then we called all 88 employees into the cafeteria and announced the acquisition. We explained Wiremold's structure and told them that their business would now report to Bob Ahlstrom. We gave a brief overview of Wiremold's history and culture, and welcomed them to our profit-sharing program. There was a coffee break, and then we brought them back to the cafeteria, where I gave a $2\frac{1}{2}$-hour presentation on Lean and the Wiremold production process. By then it was time for lunch. Before we let them go, we posted the names of the people who were going to be on the first two *kaizen* teams. We explained the two areas where we would be working after lunch, and we told them that I would lead one team and that Bob Ahlstrom would lead the other. We told everyone else just to go back to work, but to plan on being on a *kaizen* team before too long.

After lunch, we started our first two *kaizen* events, which were scheduled to run until the end of the week. I was working on a conveyer belt assembly line about 100 feet long, one of four such lines used for final assembly. The team started by calculating *takt* time and then doing time observations on the current process. We discussed what was value-added and what was non-value-added. By 4 p.m., I had them disconnect the entire assembly line, hook it up to a couple of forklift trucks, and put it out in the backyard to be thrown away.

The employees had been using a moving assembly line for many years, so watching it be hauled off and dumped out back was a shock. We watched it go for a moment, then forged ahead. While the conveyor belt was being disconnected, the team created a new cellular layout that had simple benchtop equipment and incorporated one of the previous operations. This new layout called for a team of six operators instead of ten and reduced floor space by 60 percent while producing the same or slightly more product. Then it was time to go to dinner.

At dinner, Mike Babasick, the plant manager—a very likable guy who was on my *kaizen* team—asked if he still had to write the 20-page monthly plant report that he had been sending to the prior owners. If he was somehow addicted to this report, he could keep writing it, we said, but we were not going to read it. Spend your time on the shop floor creating flow, I said. He did. Over the next year, he produced the results shown in Table 10.4.

Table 10.4   Results for Dual Light

	1997	1998	% Change
Space	100%	40%	−60%
Inventory	100%	50%	−50%
Head count	88	55	−38%*
Operating profit	Loss	14%	N/A

*All by attrition.

When we finally consolidated this plant into our California operations, Mike Babasick, the plant manager, was promoted to vice president of operations for the combined business. He continued implementing Lean and did an excellent job, even though he never wrote another monthly plant report.

Over the course of 10 years, I led 21 acquisitions at Wiremold, absorbing new product lines and businesses and adding strategic new businesses around the world, and all of the transitions were substantially the same. Some people needed more convincing than others, and we sometimes ran into unforeseen issues. But across the board, we told people that Wiremold was Lean and that they would be Lean; we showed them how to become Lean and began improving the business.

The key point is that Lean not only lowers the risk of acquisition by increasing the rate at which money is returned, but also offers a clear game plan on how to proceed with the transition. There is no ambiguity for either party. People are told what to expect and then given the tools to make it happen. Having the CEO of a new parent company spend a week—or several weeks—on the shop floor gives new associates the opportunity to ask questions and remove any doubts about their direction. New employees quickly learn that Lean focuses on processes, not people, and is always aimed at making work easier through waste reduction. In one noisy, dirty, waste-filled plant after another, we found that people were eager to make these changes.

Of course, many people will be skeptical of Lean at first. But starting immediately with *kaizen* projects led by the new CEO breaks down the natural resistance to change. Before you know it, you have an organization that is moving quickly down the Lean path, helping to generate excess earnings and cash flow to help finance the next acquisition. Lean is the gift that keeps on giving.

Lean Everywhere

All companies, whether manufacturing or nonmanufacturing, are alike. They are all composed of a series of processes that, taken together, allow them to do what they do as a business. In fact, certain processes, such as hiring, ordering, accounting, invoicing, and similar functions, are common to both types. Lean provides big financial gains to any company by focusing on improving every process to remove the waste and allow value to flow to the customers. As a result, it works its magic equally as well in nonmanufacturing companies as it does in manufacturers. This has not been lost on the hospital industry, where many organizations have started a Lean transformation. The main point is that Lean strategy can help any company, no matter what it does.

Would you call a plumber to paint your kitchen? If you ran a hospital or an insurance company, and you wanted to try to improve the way you did things, would calling in someone who made automobiles or toaster ovens be the first thing that came to mind? Of course not. People don't think that way. What something is called is usually descriptive of what it is. There are exceptions, of course. For example, comedian Stephen Wright asks the question, "Ever wonder why we park in a driveway and drive on a parkway?" So if you call something "Lean manufacturing," it will conjure up some thought in your mind about what this is.

As I discussed earlier, this terminology (and it is the most common way to refer to Lean) is unfortunate even for manufacturing companies. Their boards, CEOs, and senior staff members miss the strategic aspect of Lean completely. They use Lean only as a way to cut costs or cut inventory. In addition, it is easy to understand why something called "Lean manufacturing" has gotten very little traction in nonmanufacturing environments. This is a real pity, because the truth is that as big as the gains from Lean can be in manufacturing companies, they usually can be even bigger in nonmanufacturing environments.

Now if we called it "Lean strategy" or even "Lean management," it would be much easier for nonmanufacturing companies to at least try to understand how it could help them. Certainly the idea of continuous improvement, or eliminating waste to let value flow to your customers faster and more cheaply, should not be objectionable in any company.

I believe that all companies, when you break them down, are alike in the things that matter most. It doesn't matter whether they are manufacturers, distributors, or service companies. They are all composed of a series of processes that are the basis on which they do business. Many of these processes (order entry, purchasing, billing, collections, computer systems, human resource systems, and so on) are common across all types of companies. In addition, almost every type of company today continues to do its work using some form of batch approach. Manufacturers have functional departments based upon similar types of machines, while service companies have fiefdoms based upon the way they have divided up the work to be done.

Using Lean to remove waste by attacking and improving every process creates huge gains from letting value flow better, based on the demand of the customer (i.e., *takt* time). Because all companies are made up of multiple processes, then, Lean really is a perfect fit for every company.

The gains from Lean tend to be bigger in nonmanufacturing companies for a number of reasons. First of all, most manufacturers have put a lot of effort over the years into trying to improve their productivity by

improving the way they make things. More important, in a manufacturing environment, you can physically go and observe the work on the shop
floor. In service-type companies, on the other hand, you can't really see
the work. It happens on people's desks on different floors and in different
departments. In addition, there hasn't been as much emphasis on improving the value-adding work itself; more than likely, the emphasis has just
been on automating the existing waste. Service companies seem to really
love big, complicated (i.e., expensive) computer systems. As a result, just
trying to understand what the actual process is can be very difficult in a
service company. There is also much more resistance to any type of
change from the workforce in a service company. Associates consider
themselves "experts" at their jobs and don't think anyone else can do what
they do as well as they can.

When you do begin to investigate the processes in a service company,
you will see huge potential gains. Seeing this requires you to go back to the
Lean fundamentals that we talked about earlier: *takt* time, one-piece flow,
standard work, and connecting to the customer through pull. Creating a
value-stream map so that you can look at what is being done through the
takt time lens, for example, can be particularly enlightening. At Wiremold,
we made big gains in productivity in such areas as accounting, order entry,
purchasing, quoting, warehousing, and shipping, all of which exist in many
types of service companies or distributors.

Look for processes and practices that are similar, not the things that
are different. For example, when Gary Kaplan, CEO of Virginia Mason
Medical Center (VMMC) in Seattle, Washington, started his Lean journey, he flew 30 of his key managers and doctors from Seattle to Hartford,
Connecticut, to spend a couple of days with Wiremold. The main thrust
of this visit was to see if they could understand what we did in a manufacturing environment that was similar to what they did and could
therefore be transferred back to Virginia Mason.

We started them out with a simple concept. We explained that in our
business, we began with a piece of steel or plastic (our raw material).
We then moved it through a series of processes where we drilled holes

in it, attached things to it, wrapped it up, put it in a box, and sold it to a customer. Their business, we explained, was exactly the same. They started with a human body (the raw material), moved it through various processes where they drilled holes in it, attached things to it, bandaged it up, put it in a car (no box, please), and sent it home. They got a few laughs out of this analogy, but at the same time they understood that this was basically true. What we did and what they did were fundamentally the same.

We spent the rest of our time together showing them how we moved our raw material through the shop. We explained how our gains came from removing the waste—all the time that our parts spent lying around waiting—and letting the raw material flow directly into the box. They could easily relate this to their own situation, where their patients (i.e., raw material) spent endless hours waiting and being moved around so that value could be added to improve their condition sufficiently that they could finally get in the car and go home.

This was a great visit. We all had fun, and we learned a lot from each other. Virginia Mason had brought its A team, so when they went home, they were all on the same page. Today, I believe that Virginia Mason is the leader in the United States in applying Lean in a hospital. After leaving Wiremold, the team went to visit Toyota plants in Japan for a graduate course in Lean. Even today, one of the requirements for being a Virginia Mason director is that you have to spend a week in Japan visiting advanced Lean practitioners. This has given the hospital a strong Lean-centric board. In fact, one of the board members, Carolyn Corvi, was formerly the head of operations for Boeing's Commercial Airplanes business and is one of the best Lean practitioners in the United States.

Lean in Hospitals

Perhaps the best way to help you understand how well Lean works in non-manufacturing companies is to provide you with a few examples. Lean is rapidly taking hold in U.S. hospitals these days. This is an industry that is getting squeezed from all sides: the government (Medicare and Medicaid) and the insurance companies on the revenue side, and rising costs for everything they do. Hospitals have to improve how they do everything or risk going out of business. I have been helping one of the largest hospitals in Hartford, Connecticut, Saint Francis Medical Center, get started with a Lean turnaround and have led a number of *kaizen* projects at the hospital. As a result, I have a lot of firsthand insight here.

Let's start with a quick overview of how a hospital is organized. Just as traditional manufacturing organizations are organized into functional departments based on equipment type, hospitals are organized into silos based on what type of work is done or what treatment is given. For a patient to get treated, the patient has to pass through (across) numerous silos. For example, if you go to the hospital with a broken leg, you might have to pass through (1) the emergency room silo, (2) the admissions silo, (3) the x-ray silo, (4) the blood lab silo, (5) the transport silo, (6) the operating room silo, (7) the anesthesiology silo, (8) the operating room nurse silo, (9) the ward or floor nurse silo, (10) the kitchen silo, (11) the pharmacy silo, (12) the orthopedic silo, and (13) the discharge silo. Each of these silos functions as its own fiefdom. They might even have different computer systems that, of course, aren't compatible with each other. They each have their own rules on how they do things. Even so, it's important for you that when they do talk to each other, they get it right. Miscommunication in hospitals (e.g., the wrong medication given) can kill you.

Add to this the fact that in most hospitals, the doctors are not employees, but rather independent contractors who have a right to practice at that particular hospital. What this means is that most hospitals treat the doctors as their sales force. The doctors are the ones that go out and get the patients and bring them into the hospital. This means that the hospital is quite reliant on the doctors for its revenue stream. As a result, it tends to bend over backward to accommodate the doctors' wishes. That might be okay if it were done within a rigid Lean structure at the hospital itself. The problem, of course, is that this is rarely the case, and trying to accommodate every doctor creates lots of duplication, waste, and excess expenses.

Because of all the silos and the accommodations, it is not surprising that there is not much flow in your typical hospital. The patient gets moved all over the place to get things done and spends a majority of the time lying in the hallway staring at the ceiling. Add to that the fact that most large hospitals (particularly those in the inner city) are constrained by available space. As a result, they get built in a hodgepodge way over time. Thus, the different treatments that might occur within an overall medical specialty are spread randomly throughout the hospital. There is no thinking in terms of value streams, and even if you did think that way, you would face physical constraints.

Even so, the concept of value-stream organizations clearly applies to hospitals. As an example, you could have a value stream for the heart. In a $500 million per year hospital, it would not be uncommon to find that when you added up all the treatments that were done relating to the heart, this would be a $100 to $125 million business. At this size, you could have a value-stream leader who was responsible for the total heart business, which would include making improvements in patient care, patient satisfaction, flow, cost, patient movement, wait time, and time spent in the hospital, and, of course, making sure that the total heart business was profitable.

Instead, today you will find that treatments related to the heart are done by several different specialist groups: cardiologists, cardiac surgeons, cardiology PAs (physician's assistants), and cardiac nurses. Nobody is in charge of the overall value stream. The potential gains from linking everything together are huge. I'm sure that many of the hospitals that have started down the Lean path have already come to this conclusion and are working on creating logical value streams.

I know that every time I have run a *kaizen* at the hospital, the very first day, when I have the team together, I always ask the question, "What is your biggest problem?" The answer I get is always the same: "It's the doctors!" This is usually followed by a list of detailed complaints.

My response, however, is always the same: "Look, there are 5,000 people that work in this hospital, and only 500 of them are doctors. So let's focus on improving what the other 4,500 are doing, and I guarantee you that we can get the doctors to fall in line." This, by the way, has always been true.

The very first *kaizen* I did at the hospital concerned the cathology lab (in fact, there were three separate rooms where heart cauterizations were done). I didn't know anything about heart cauterizations at the beginning of the week. But then again, I wasn't planning to do one, so it didn't matter. The problem the hospital was having was that the cath lab was working so much overtime that it couldn't keep any full-time staff. It was mostly using contract "traveling" nurses who cost about 1.5 times what a normal local nurse would cost, and it was worried about a lack of capacity. When I asked what was the biggest problem, people of course said, "It's the doctors." When I asked for specifics, I was told, "They don't show up on time." The people on the team said that there was a daily schedule for each lab, but when I asked what percentage of the time the labs ran on schedule, the answer was, "Only about 20 percent of the time." I then asked, "Well, then, why are you surprised that the doctors don't show up on time? I wouldn't and neither would you if you knew in advance that the labs were hardly ever ready on time."

It turned out that the doctors were the most consistent part of the whole thing. Just about all of them could repeatedly do a cath procedure in 45 minutes. With that as a given, we talked about *takt* time, one-piece flow, standard work, and pull. As we dug in and got the data on each one, it became clear where we could save time, eliminate waste, and make things flow. For example, taking the basic information on a patient (which took about 10 to 15 minutes) was done three times: once by admitting, then by the nurses on the cath floor when the patient was assigned a bed, and then again by the nurses in the cath lab itself. When I asked the cath lab nurses about this, they said they "didn't trust" the information coming from the other two sources. The real problem turned out to be the lack of any type of flow. Using the Lean fundamentals, we were able to solve all these problems and prove that the cath labs could generate an extra $500,000 per year in revenue for the hospital without having to work any overtime. This, of course, would eliminate the need for expensive "traveling" nurses and save the hospital a lot of money as well.

The truth is that establishing flow has the highest of all returns for a hospital. One of the early hospital *kaizen* projects I did was focused on "bed turnover." This was really a flow exercise, as it dealt with how to increase the utilization of the hospital's fixed number of beds. The solution here was very simple: eliminate the waste and create a smooth flow for every patient from arrival to departure. I set a target of improving bed turnover by 25 percent, which proved to be quite doable. Based on the calculations done during the *kaizen*, this would generate an extra $60 million in operating income for this $500 million hospital, a significant gain with almost no capital cost involved.

Later on, I did a *kaizen* focusing on creating a discharge policy for the cardiac care unit. This was the floor that took care of patients after they had open-heart surgery. The current state was that there was no discharge policy, which meant that patients stayed too long, and when they did go home, they went home too late in the day. Once again, the solution to this problem was contained in the four Lean fundamentals. There was a clear, repeatable *takt* time for post-op recovery already (although the hospital staff didn't think in those terms). When we combined this with one-piece flow and standard work, we were able to save the hospital an estimated $1.5 million per year just by having a more structured discharge procedure.

Virginia Mason Medical Center, Seattle

Virginia Mason began its Lean journey toward the end of 2001 with the visit to Wiremold mentioned previously. Recently, it was one of only two hospitals in the United States to earn the title "Top Hospital of the Decade" from the Leapfrog Group rating organization (Leapfrog is a coalition of public and private purchasers of employee health benefits).

This is quite an honor, and it is well-deserved. The accomplishments of the VMMC team over this time period are too great to fully cover here. A sampling, however, should provide you with plenty of proof that Lean works in nonmanufacturing environments.

VMMC Selected Accomplishments

- VMMC nurses spend 90 percent of their time with patients versus 35 percent at an average hospital.
- Time to report lab test results to patients dropped 85 percent.
- Cost of supplies was cut by $1 million per year.
- Professional liability costs were down 48.9 percent.
- Hospital accounts receivable (A/R) days' outstanding greater than 90 days decreased 74 percent.
- Changes in the spine clinic: space was down 78 percent, head count was down 29 percent, and margin was up 56 percent.
- Changes in the surgery center: case time (cut to close plus setup) was down 39 percent, case turnover (out to in) was down 50 percent, and cases per day per OR increased from 5 to 8, or 60 percent.
- For the pharmacy medication distribution, order to available, was down 93 percent.

The list could go on and on, but the bottom line is that VMMC was able to increase its overall margin dollars per year from $700,000 in the year 2000 to $40.9 million in 2010. This illustrates that Lean provides not only better patient outcomes but better financial results as well.

Sheridan Healthcare, Inc.

Sheridan is a leader in medical practice management, supplying physicians in such specialties as anesthesiology, neonatology, radiology, and emergency room doctors to approximately 200 hospitals in 20 states.

It is a former J. W. Childs Associates portfolio company, and it began its Lean journey in 2005 while a part of the J. W. Childs family. Its CEO, Dr. Mitchell Eisenberg, is a very forward-thinking individual, and he quickly understood that a Lean strategy could really help his business. Sheridan started in the accounts receivable department and got tremendous results; A/R days' outstanding were reduced by 15 days, errors were cut by 50 percent, and productivity increased by 30 percent. Sheridan has since expanded Lean into everything it does. Here are some examples.

Emergency Department 1
- Time from in bed to physician greet went from 12 min. to 6 min., down 50 percent.

Emergency Department 2
- Average length of stay went from 250 min. to 179 min., down 30 percent.

Anesthesia Department 1
- Surgery cancel rate within 24 hours of start decreased from 19 percent to 5 percent, down 74 percent.

Anesthesia Department 2
- Non-value-adding time went from 80 min. to 40 min., down 50 percent.
- Walking distance went from 8,400 ft. to 2,625 ft., down 69 percent.
- Overall cycle time went from 123 min. to 70 min., down 43 percent.

These are great results, but the most important thing is, how does the leadership of the company view them? Sheridan's president, Bob Coward, explains it this way: "Everything we do, we can do better and faster, and without adding resources, because we use Lean tools to drive out waste. We continue to learn how to improve. And we can leverage our operational excellence into growth, not only because we have a better reputation, but we have a more agile and robust solution capacity backed by real measures of quality, turnaround time, and productivity. We can prove our value to our customers and are differentiated from our competition because we can actually deliver on the promises we make." I couldn't have said it better.

Lean in Life Insurance

I live in Avon, Connecticut, which is just outside of Hartford, one of the major insurance hubs in the United States. As a result, it shouldn't be surprising that I would get involved in applying Lean to an insurance company. I was contacted by the CEO of a midsized life company that did not have its own retail sales force (it had wholesalers and sold through outside sales forces; in this case, it sold its life policies through the retail sales force of a much larger property-casualty company).

The issue was that it took the company around 48 days to respond to an application for insurance with a quote. In some cases it took even longer, but 48 days was the average. According to the company, the rest of the industry took about 45 days to do the same thing. As a result, although the company felt that it needed to get better, it didn't feel that it was very far off. And, as you might expect, the number of reasons (i.e., excuses) why the company couldn't get better was very long. Worse than that, the heads of the underwriting and case management departments firmly believed in the list of excuses.

In the first *kaizen* I was involved in, I established a goal of responding in 5 days, not 48. The people on the team didn't like that too much, but at least it forced them to think about the problem in a totally different way. I then asked them how long it takes an underwriter to underwrite a life once he had in his possession all of the information needed to do the underwriting. They had no idea. I made them take a guess. They said two to four hours, but it would vary depending on the type of insurance and the face value of the policy.

I asked them to get 10 policies that had all of the information needed to complete the underwriting, and I had them time how long it took the underwriter to do the underwriting. The answer was between 9 and 12 minutes, and neither the type of policy nor its size seemed to matter. I rounded this up to 15 minutes per life. This meant that as long as an underwriter had all the information available, he could underwrite 150 lives per week. On the few occasions when a physician's statement was needed, the underwriting would take longer, so we set the target at 100 to 125 lives per week.

Once I had this information, of course, I asked, "How many lives per week does an underwriter do now?" The answer was 15. Wow! So now we knew that not only were we too slow, but we were also incredibly unproductive. The solution again used the four Lean fundamentals: *takt* time, one-piece flow, standard work, and pull. We set up a simple cell with four case managers and one underwriter sitting very close to each other in an open space. (They hated that—it wasn't professional; underwriters needed to be in their own department.) The job of each case manager was to hand the underwriter one fully completed case (i.e., for which all the information needed was present) per hour. I then had them set up a visual board to track how many cases were underwritten each hour versus their target of four. (They really hated that.)

At the end of the day, despite massive resistance at every turn, we got to where more than half the applications were being responded to with a quote in less than 20 days (which also provided the path to the 5-day goal) and the underwriter was doing about 88 lives per week (almost six times as many as before, but still with a lot of upside). Unfortunately, the financial crisis took a big toll on this company, and it had to stop offering these policies, so this was as far as we got. I don't know if we would have hit the 5-day target, but I was convinced that 10 days was very doable, as was more than 100 lives per week per underwriter. In any event, I think we proved that a Lean strategy can do wonders for a life insurance company.

Lean in a Distributor/Retailer

One of the main functions of an industrial distributor (or a retailer, for that matter) is managing its warehouse. These firms buy products from various manufacturers, then resell those products to the end user. (The retailer, of course, adds the step of having to display the goods.) At Wiremold, we sold through electrical distributors, all of whom had to run and manage a warehouse (or, in many cases, multiple warehouses). We had two warehouses ourselves, and we had been applying Lean to them as well. We picked by zone or size and not by order. This was much more efficient, reduced the amount of space we needed, and virtually eliminated errors. As we perfected this, my goal was to begin to teach our distributors how to do this as well as a sort of extra value-added service they got as a result of doing business with us. Unfortunately, I retired before this became a reality.

I have, however, continued this zone-picking push in my portfolio companies as a partner at J. W. Childs Associates, L.P. One of my consumer products companies, Company E, is furthest down this path. It has been able to achieve the following in one of its European distribution centers:

Zone-Picking Results

1. Reduced head count from 16.5 to 9.5, down 42 percent.
2. Freed up 35,000 sq. ft. of space, saving $180,000 per year.
3. Increased the number of picks per 10 feet of rack from 9 to 42, an increase of 367 percent.
4. Reduced shipping errors from 1.1 percent to 0.11 percent, a decrease of 90 percent.

These are the types of gains that any warehouse operation can expect from making the switch to a Lean turnaround. I could cite other nonmanufacturing examples, but I think you get the picture. Lean applies to any type of company, and in fact, the gains in nonmanufacturing environments are usually bigger than those in manufacturing.

So What Are You Waiting For?

By now I hope you see how any company, in any industry, can be turned around (i.e., dramatically improved) by implementing a Lean strategy. I've learned from experience that companies can grow and increase in value only by delivering more value to their customers over long periods of time than their competitors can. And I want you to see that in order to deliver value to your customers, you must first improve your own value-adding activities by continuously removing the waste that exists in every one of your processes. A Lean strategy, and the Lean tools that come with it, will allow you to "see" the waste that exists and enable you to remove it quickly and efficiently.

As your value-adding activities improve, the amount of time it takes for each of your processes will be dramatically reduced. This will also lower your costs and improve your quality, but, most important, it will allow you to compete on time and thus deliver more value to your customers. Your ability to respond quickly and reliably to your customers' requests will set you apart from your competition. This will allow you to grow your market share, secure the jobs of your employees, and increase your enterprise value.

Why Isn't Everyone Doing This?

The results from a Lean turnaround will always speak for themselves. You should easily be able to equal or exceed the Wiremold results shown here, as they are pretty typical of what many other companies have achieved in their own Lean turnaround.

The Wiremold Company 1991–2000

- Lead time dropped from 4 to 6 weeks to 1 to 2 days.
- Customer service went from 50 percent to 98 percent.
- Productivity went up 162 percent.
- Sales quadrupled.
- EBITDA margin went from 6.2 percent to 20.8 percent.
- Gross profit went from 38 percent to 51 percent.
- Working capital/sales decreased from 21.8 percent to 6.7 percent.
- Machine changeovers went from 3 per week to 20 to 30 per day.
- Operating income went up 13.4 times.
- Inventory turns went from 3 times to 18 times.
- Enterprise value went up 2,467 percent.

I'm sure that your shareholders will not complain if you increase the value of their stock by 2,467 percent, as shown here. As the leader of a business, the ability to get these types of results from implementing a Lean strategy ought to provide all the incentive you need to rush out and implement your own Lean turnaround. Unfortunately, this is not the case.

Given this proof, why isn't everyone doing this? This is the question that anyone who has successfully implemented Lean over any length of time (30 years in my case) always asks. There are two main barriers here, both of which we cover in this book. The first is a general lack of understanding of Lean and Lean strategy. People don't understand the Lean tools or how this approach differs from the traditional management approach (make the month, focus on the numbers) that all of us have grown up with. To make matters worse, Lean has commonly become known as "Lean manufacturing." This is tragic, as it allows even manufacturing companies to view it as some "manufacturing thing." Thus, they try to delegate it to their vice president of operations to see if he can cut head count or lower inventory. They can't see Lean, and the Lean tools, for what it really is: the greatest strategic weapon that any company can have.

This is an even bigger problem for nonmanufacturing companies, where the gains from implementing a Lean strategy are almost always greater than those in manufacturing companies. If you refer to something as "Lean manufacturing," I guess it should not be surprising that most companies outside of manufacturing don't think it applies to them and never even consider it. Even so, there are some great examples of tremendous gains being made in nonmanufacturing companies; Virginia Mason Medical Center in Seattle, led by CEO Gary Kaplan and his great team, is a prime example.

The second and more important reason why companies are not using a Lean strategy to achieve a Lean turnaround of their companies is a lack of leadership. CEOs have been trained in traditional management, they are busy, and because the Lean approach will require a 180-degree change in the way they do everything, it seems like too big a change to even attempt. The idea that with Lean, "the winners will be those that focus on their processes, not their results" is probably too big a leap of faith for a CEO who has been trained to spend a good portion of his time focusing on results. Yet one thing is very clear: you can't have a Lean turnaround if the CEO (or the business owner, division president, plant or regional manager, or whoever has the leadership role) won't lead it. Trying to help CEOs overcome this reluctance, then, is the main thrust of this book. If nothing else, it is a game plan for how a CEO can successfully lead a Lean turnaround.

I know firsthand how hard this can be. My first exposure to Lean came during my first general manager job at the General Electric

Company. Talk about traditional; back then, it was "make the month or die," about as far from Lean as you could get. At the same time, Lean made more sense to me, and as I moved on to a group executive role at Danaher Corporation, I was lucky enough to have great Lean *sensei* who had worked for Taiichi Ohno at Toyota. They forced me to learn and taught me how to look at things totally differently. The more I learned, the more my management style changed. I went from a GE manager guy to more of a leader and coach. My world was upside down because Lean is almost the polar opposite of traditional management. Even so, it just made so much sense that I never questioned that this indeed was a better way. My management style evolved naturally as my understanding grew, and so will yours.

Getting Started: Some CEO Musts

Before leading a Lean turnaround, the CEO must understand three key management principles or guidelines.

- Lean is the strategy.
- Lead from the top.
- Transform the people.

Lean, or continuous improvement of all your processes and value-adding activities, has to be at the core of what you are doing. This is what I mean by "Lean is the strategy." It doesn't mean that you have to stop doing what you now think of as strategy. It will just give you a much better chance of being successful as well as adding new strategic options that you don't have now. For example, if you cut your cycle time to make a product from 6 weeks to 20 minutes (a very common occurrence with Lean), you can cut your lead time to the customer and gain market share without having to carry lots of inventory. You wouldn't have this option if you let the cycle time stay at 6 weeks.

As mentioned previously, you cannot have a Lean turnaround if the CEO won't lead it (not manage it) in an out-front, hands-on way. So get out of your office (no value-adding is occurring there) and go to your *gemba* (workplace)! Remember that what you are trying to transform is your people. They are the only asset you have that can appreciate over time, and they will have the best ideas of how to improve your value-adding activities (they are the ones who are doing the work).

The next hurdle is getting the Lean knowledge you will need in order to implement a Lean turnaround in your company. You don't have to start out as a Lean expert in order to be successful, but you do have to commit to becoming one. Start by learning and committing to the following Lean fundamentals. They will serve as the guideposts for your turnaround. You have to insist that all of these are implemented in your company.

Lean Fundamentals

- Work to *takt* time
- One-piece flow
- Standard work
- Connect the customer to the work by using a pull system

Takt time measures the rate of customer demand. It will connect you to your customers and will be the principal tool in helping you to "see" all the waste in your value-adding activities. One-piece flow (or flow) is what will allow you to eliminate the waste that the *takt* time tool will help you see. It is also the key to productivity and quality improvements. Standard work provides the consistency and base on which to further improve. Pull systems or *kanban* allows you to connect directly to the demand of your customers in the least waste way, "sell one—make one."

Next Steps: Implementing Lean

As the Lean leader, you will be very busy. You will need to create a simple Lean strategy (vision) that articulates the stretch goals that will drive your turnaround. You will also need to develop the company core values that will help you make the transition to Lean being your company culture. Companies with a true Lean culture (i.e., "this is the way we do things here") are very hard to beat. That's why you don't just want to *do* Lean; you want to *be* Lean.

You will need to do some value-stream mapping (especially if you are a service company) to identify your value streams, and I would highly recommend that you introduce policy deployment (*hoshin kanri*) early on as your planning tool to get everyone (especially your management team) going in the same direction. You'll need to organize around your value streams so that your *kaizen* activities can focus on your value-adding activities and there will be a management structure in place to follow up and hold onto the gains of the *kaizen* projects. One of the biggest mistakes I see companies make is to try to implement Lean without changing their functional/silo organizational structure. You need a value-stream organization if you are to be successful.

As you start your aggressive *kaizen* activity, you, personally, should do the initial training of your people. You should be heavily involved in picking the initial *kaizen* projects and setting the stretch targets for each one. As you move along, your role will intensify. You need to be the company's Lean "zealot" who keeps everything on track and moving forward (your people will tend to fall backward if you don't). Focus first on implementing flow and standard work, and then try to connect your new processes to your customers and vendors with a robust pull system.

You will need to implement a strong daily management system to keep everything on track, and you will need to support this with daily visits to your value-adding activities. You should also set up a monthly tracking system at the plant and company level to measure your progress on your key Lean measurements (e.g., customer service, quality, productivity, inventory turns, visual management, and 5S).

Dump the Bad and Leverage the Good

As you switch to Lean, you will have to get rid of most of your traditional measurements, like direct to indirect head count. You will also need to get rid of your standard-cost accounting system early in your Lean journey. Standard-cost systems don't provide very good management information in the first place (just lots of useless variance analysis), but, more important, they reward all the bad practices (like building inventory) that you are trying to get rid of.

As your Lean turnaround progresses, you can start to leverage your new Lean processes and value-adding activities in the marketplace. Introduce Quality Function Deployment (QFD) to reduce your product development cycle by 50 to 70 percent and get the "voice of the customer" into your new product designs. Shorten your lead times and make it easier for customers to do business with you. Leverage your customers' measurements of their vendors to your advantage by helping them reduce inventory and delivering to them more frequently. And don't forget acquisitions. Lean gives you many advantages in doing acquisitions; it provides the cash, lowers the risk, and gives you a clear game plan. Take advantage of it.

The Lean turnaround will leverage any business. One of the more active industries in implementing Lean in the United States at the moment is hospitals. They are under pressure from all sides, but they are getting great gains from their Lean activities. The opportunities in this sector, as well as among insurance companies, banks, wholesalers, and a whole host of other service companies, are far greater than in manufacturing. I hope more leaders will adopt a Lean strategy, follow the guidelines laid out in this book, and complete a successful Lean turnaround. I promise that you will learn more and have more fun doing this than anything you have ever done before.

So let's go! Don't be afraid; get out there and start your own Lean turnaround. After all, you are the leader of your operation. Don't you want to get better?

I've been doing this for more than 30 years in many different companies and countries, and I have enjoyed the same successes every time. In case you didn't notice, I am very passionate about this way of working, and I want you all to be just as passionate. You owe it to your employees and your stakeholders to make your operation the best it can be. If you don't agree, you are in the wrong job. Respect your people, tap into their knowledge, grow your market share, and create wealth for all your stakeholders. Take the Lean leap. You'll never enjoy anything more than this. Every company can be turned around using the Lean approach. Have fun, and send me some e-mails about your success stories. I know that there will be lots of them. You can contact me at abyrne@jwchilds.com.

Lean Resources

Books

Many books have been written on Lean in general and on all the Lean tools. In keeping with the managerial thrust of this book, I am recommending only the books that I think you, as the leader of your business, would get the most out of.

Cunningham, Jean E., and Orest J. Fiume, with Emily Adams, *Real Numbers: Management Accounting in a Lean Organization*. Durham, NC: Managing Times Press, 2003.

Emiliani, Bob. *Better Thinking, Better Results: Case Study and Analysis of an Enterprise-Wide Lean Transformation*, 2nd. ed. Kensington, CT: Center for Lean Business Management, 2003.

Imai, Masaaki. *Gemba Kaizen: A Commonsense Approach to a Continuous Improvement Strategy*, 2nd. ed. New York: McGraw-Hill, 2012.

Ohno, Taiichi. *Toyota Production System: Beyond Large-Scale Production*. Portland, OR: Productivity Press, 1988.

Rother, Mike, and John Shook. *Learning to See: Value Stream Mapping to Add Value and Eliminate MUDA*. Brookline, MA: Lean Enterprise Institute, 1999.

Shingo, Shigeo. *A Study of the Toyota Production System: From an Industrial Engineering Viewpoint*. Portland, OR: Productivity Press, 1981.

Womack, James P., Daniel T. Jones, and Daniel Roos. *Lean Thinking: Banish Waste and Create Wealth in Your Corporation*, 2nd ed. New York: Free Press, 2003.

Consultants

Just as in the list of books, I have tried to provide you with a limited list of Lean consultants with whom I have had personal experience and whom I can recommend without reservation. The Shingijutsu consultants are mentioned a number of times in this book, as I have been working with them since 1987. Along the way, they managed to split into two separate companies, one led by Kumi Otaka (daughter of Yoshiki Iwata, the first president and a founder of Shingijutsu) and the other led by Chihiro Nakao (another founder of the original company). I have provided contact information for both.

The other firm that I have had a lot of experience with is Moffitt Associates, which is headed by Jim Cutler. I have used this firm at Wiremold and in all of our portfolio companies at J. W. Childs Associates, L.P. I also have had experience with all of the other firms listed, and I believe you will be well served by them.

Shingijutsu Consulting Company. Contact Chihiro Nakao at c.nakao@ shingijutsu.co.jp.

Shingijutsu Global Consulting. Contact Kumi Iwata Otake at office@ shingijutsu-global.com. Phone: (425) 451–8651.

DD Consulting LLC. Contact Don Doles at dondoles45@ gmail.com.

Lean Horizons Consulting. Contact Mark Deluzio at mark.Deluzio@ leanhorizons.com. Phone: (860) 430–1174.

Moffitt Associates, L.P. Contact Jim Cutler at cutassoc@aol.com. Phone: (847) 604–8412.

Simpler Consulting. Contact Mark Hafer at haferm@simpler.com. Phone: (336) 918–1923.

Strategy Deployment Services, LLC. Very good for strategy deployment and *hoshin kanri*. Contact Ed Miller at infor@strategydevelop.com. Phone: (860) 675–1448.

TBM Consulting Group. Contact Anand Sharma at (800) 438–5535.

Executive Search Services

When you are looking for staff for your *kaizen* promotion office (KPO), you have many executive search firms to choose from. Very few, however, specialize in Lean/Six Sigma executive search. The leading firm in this specialized area is Stiles Associates, LLC. Contact Jake Stiles at (603) 526–6566.

Notes

Introduction

1. *Kaizen*, a term that I use a lot, is a Japanese word for "making something better." As used by Toyota Motors, it refers to the idea of continuous improvement. A *kaizen* culture is no more than a continuous improvement culture. *Kaizen* can also be used to refer to an improvement activity, such as a week-long *kaizen* event or workshop. The *kaizen* office refers to a function within a company that is responsible for continuous improvement activities, such as the *kaizen* promotion office, or KPO.

2. This is a key distinction between traditional ways of operating and doing things the Lean way. The most common way for any company—whether manufacturing or service or healthcare—to do its work (i.e., add value) is to do it in batches. All the applications, for example, go to Department A, where they stay until they are all done, at which point they all move on to Departments B, C, D, E, and so on. Or in manufacturing, we may make red ones the first week of the month, then spend two weeks making blue ones, and then one week making green ones. This tends to extend the time it takes to get a finished product and also hides all the waste in the process. A flow approach, on the other hand, organizes the work in such a way that once an application or product is started, it doesn't stop or get put down until it is completed. This has the opposite effect of a batch approach because it exposes waste and shortens lead times.

3. *Gemba* is a Japanese term that refers to the workplace or worksite. This can be any location (office, factory, growing fields, and so on) where the actual work takes place.

Chapter 1

1. *Kanban* is essentially a card or a visual cue that tells associates to produce or replenish the required parts or products in the proper amount. *Kanban* is derived from the Japanese word for "signboard."

2. *Hoshin*, or *hoshin kanri*, refers to the process of policy deployment. *Hoshin kanri* is a visual planning process that focuses on the most important priorities and aligns company resources around those priorities. This work is conducted within the context of the longer-term strategic plan, and it clearly defines the current-year projects (or *hoshins*) that need to be done. A *hoshin* team leader is assigned to head up one of these projects. (See Chapter 7 for a more detailed explanation of policy deployment.)

Chapter 4

1. Quality function deployment (QFD) is a Lean approach to planning new products and services. It uses a visual method to align the customer's wants and needs to determine what the priorities should be. It also gets the "voice of the customer" into the planning process up front, which helps ensure acceptance of the new product or service. This process is a must for any type of company.

Chapter 5

1. MRP refers to material resource planning (MRP) computer systems that are commonly used by manufacturers, distributors, retailers, and others to determine when to purchase components or finished products and when to schedule production. They are generally used in a "batch" approach, in anticipation of demand as opposed to responding to demand.
2. *Value-stream structure* refers to a company that is organized by product family or by the flow of the value-adding activities required to provide a product or service. For example, a hospital may have a value stream for everything related to the heart, or for everything related to orthopedics. A life insurer may link together everything needed to receive and review an application, including underwriting it and issuing a policy.

Chapter 8

1. I borrowed this P&L from a 2006 presentation by former Wiremold CFO Orry Fiume. Similar examples appear in the book *Real Numbers: Management Accounting in a Lean Organization*, coauthored with Jean E. Cunningham.
2. Figure 8.3 was again borrowed from Orry Fiume, who called it the Plain English P&L.

3. EBITDAI is EBITDA (earnings before interest, taxes, depreciation, and amortization) with the addition of the noncash charge or credit for the change in the overhead component of inventory.
4. Enterprise resource planning systems are commonly used in many industries. The rationale for these computer systems is that they link together all the other computer systems in a company so that everything can be coordinated and properly accounted for. As you might expect, this can get quite complicated.

Chapter 9

1. A production control board is a simple board (it could be a flipchart or a more sophisticated electronic monitor) that displays the hour-by-hour production targets and the actual results for each hour, along with comments on why the target was missed (or exceeded) in any particular hour. This can be used for any manufacturing process or service and is applicable to all companies.

Chapter 10

1. Working capital turns equals gross account receivable (no reserves), plus gross inventory (no reserves), minus trade accounts payable.

Index

About the Author

ART BYRNE has been implementing Lean in various companies (over 30 counting subsidiaries) and in multiple countries [14] for the past 30 years. He has always done this from the effective title of CEO so he has an excellent grasp of what the leader of any business needs to do to turnaround their company using a Lean strategy. Art began his Lean journey as General Manager at the General Electric Company. As Group Executive, he was instrumental at introducing Lean to the Danaher Corporation. He went on to become CEO at the Wiremold Company where he quadrupled the companies size and increased its enterprise value by 2,500 percent in just under 10 years. Under Art's leadership, Wiremold won the Shingo Prize. Today, he is an Operating Partner with J.W. Childs Associates where he has been implementing Lean throughout the Childs' portfolio companies. He also serves as a member of the Board of the Shingo Prize.